LAYING DOWN THE LAW

LAYING DOWN THE LAW

THE 25 LAWS OF PARENTING

to Keep Your Kids on Track,
Out of Trouble, and
(Pretty Much) Under Control

Dr. Ruth Peters

Contributor to NBC's *Today* Show
and Author of *Don't Be Afraid to Discipline*

RODALE

Printed in the United States of America

Rodale Inc. makes every effort to use acid-free ∞ , recycled paper ♻ .

Interior design by Leanne Coppola
Cover design by Kirk DouPonce/UDG DesignWorks
Cover photograph by Michael Hoiland

Library of Congress Cataloging-in-Publication Data

Peters, Ruth Allen.
    Laying down the law: the 25 laws of parenting to keep your kids on track, out of trouble, and (pretty much) under control / Ruth Peters.
        p.   cm.
    Includes index.
    ISBN 1–57954–585–8 hardcover
    1. Parenting.   2. Child rearing.   3. Discipline of children.   I. Title.
HQ755.8 .P456 2002
649'.1—dc21   2002006612

Distributed to the book trade by St. Martin's Press

2   4   6   8   10   9   7   5   3   1   hardcover

RODALE

WE **INSPIRE** AND **ENABLE** PEOPLE TO IMPROVE
THEIR LIVES AND THE WORLD AROUND THEM

FOR MORE OF OUR PRODUCTS
WWW.RODALESTORE.COM
(800) 848-4735

To Tim and the kids,
with my love and respect—always

CONTENTS

ACKNOWLEDGMENTS

My appreciation to the thousands of families I've worked with spanning 3 decades—for the successes, tears, and laughs we've shared. From you I've learned what makes kids tick, what drives parents nuts, and what really works to harmoniously bring families together.

A very special thank you to my literary agent—Jane Dystel—who is the real thing! And to my editors, Lou Cinquino and Stephanie Tade—thanks for your belief in the wisdom and necessity of *Laying Down the Law* and your genuine concern for kids.

INTRODUCTION:
THE PREAMBLE TO THE 25 LAWS
OF PARENTING

G o f——— yourself!" were Mitchell's only words to me when I introduced myself in the waiting room of my office. Okay, I thought, we've got a live one here.

It took every ounce of self-control not to give him a quick *back at you*! Instead, I just took a deep breath and smiled. At least his rather direct salutation was a first. I'm sure that over the years many kids have wanted to say that to me (or something along a similar vein), but have used restraint and kept it to themselves.

It was evident that this guy wasn't even going to try to con me— he was satisfied with letting me have it right between the eyes. Mom would have crawled into a crack in the floor if she could, but only shook her head and meekly tried to apologize for Mitchell's rudeness.

Okay, what do we do now? Since he refused to come back to my personal office, I asked Mitchell's mom and my secretary to wait in the file room, and I began to talk with him right there in the waiting room. At least the kid was verbal—he had no difficulty describing what a jerk his stepfather was and how his mom had turned out to be a wimp and a whiner. Mitchell also let me know that he was less than impressed with me. Few sentences were emitted without some commercial-grade cursing, and I was impressed with how many permutations of the "f" word he could come up with.

Cecelia, Mitchell's mom, had recently found a copy of the *Radical Diaries* hidden in his closet, along with assorted baggies of what turned out to be a mixture of marijuana and nutmeg, various white powders mimicking cocaine, and a stash of semi-nude printouts of

1

women obtained from the Internet. And this kid was only 13 and in the eighth grade! His list of crimes included changing grades on his latest report card, skipping school, and sneaking out of the bedroom window at night to meet his friends and smoke dope. When Mitchell was at school he displayed a very short fuse—if a teacher chided him for yakking while she was teaching or for not turning in his homework, Mitchell would get in her face verbally. He was too smart to actually hit or push a teacher, but he had no qualms about sticking it to her with his words.

At home, though, Mitchell had become more physically aggressive in the past year. Pushing his younger brother around was a daily event, and Mom was considering sending her youngest to his father's house to live until Mitchell was "fixed." Even Cecelia was becoming afraid of this kid, as he would slam his bedroom door when frustrated or raise his fist at her in anger. But he never actually hit her. Oh no, not Mitchell. As an avid reader he had become somewhat of an expert in criminal law—especially when it came to juvenile issues. He knew where he could draw the line and get away with it.

He was convinced that he could bully his Mom and little brother without consequence, since all that Mom did was yell or call his step-father or threaten to send him to military school. Mitchell knew his mother well enough to be assured that these were idle threats—she didn't have the guts to send him away, nor the money, and he was right. Step-Dad traveled, and it seemed that Mitchell's outbursts occurred mainly when he was out of town and Mom was the one supposedly in charge.

Well, Mitchell was the one really running the show, and everyone knew it. Here was a 13-year-old kid, who I would have considered handsome had it not been for the pierced nose, Goth attire and perpetual scowl on his face, making his family miserable. And, as I came to understand through my talks with Mitchell, he wasn't particularly thrilled with life either. This kid really believed that his parents had it in for him and that nothing he had done, or was currently doing, played a role in their perception. The teachers were plotting against him, the preps and the jocks were just jerks, and if his folks would only leave him alone and let him make his own decisions, he would be okay.

Over the weeks Mitchell eventually came back to my private office to talk with me, and even though he consistently threatened his mother that *this was going to be the last session*, he always showed up at the next one. Go figure. He still cursed like a sailor, but after a while his life and his behavior began to make sense to me. This young man had inadvertently been allowed and therefore *encouraged* and *trained* to be disrespectful, nasty, and irresponsible.

This behavior began following his parent's divorce, when Mom was so distracted with the financial and emotional stress that she caved in to almost all of Mitchell's demands. He'd historically been a tough cookie, rather demanding and defensive, but once he saw that she was vulnerable, the boy went in for the kill. And he was a pro—lamenting that nobody liked him would usually get his Mom's undivided attention and perhaps a trip to Toys "R" Us. Since they rarely saw their father, Mom felt sorry for both of her boys, and basically let them decide their bedtime, curfews, and the menu for the week. As Mom returned to work and was absent from the home in the afternoon, Mitchell became bolder. It wasn't unusual for him to invite friends over after school, even though no one was supposed to be allowed in the home without an adult present. He would let the answering machine take Mom's futile messages rather than pick up the phone and have to listen to her whine or nag at him about breaking house rules.

Even his stepfather, David, had given up on the kid. As he was afraid of Child Protective Services becoming involved in the family's affairs, he adamantly refrained from disciplining Mitchell. David had long since reached the end of his rope and felt that if he entered into the arguments between Mitchell and Cecelia, he might become phys-

3

ical with the kid. To prevent that from happening, David either left the house or said nothing. Needless to say, the marital relationship was more than rocky, and now David had given his wife an ultimatum—either get Mitchell's behavior under control, or he was out of there.

As I learned in my therapy sessions, David leaving would be perfectly fine with Mitchell. That would be one less adult to have to deal with, and he already had his mother well figured out and securely under his control. Mitchell liked running the show, and he even took a perverse glee in intimidating his brother and mother. He also enjoyed being viewed as somewhat weird at school—some kids were afraid of him and the other Goths seemed to accept him.

But Mitchell was becoming depressed. As it turned out, not only was he reading literature such as the *Radical Diaries*, chock-full of instructions on how to make bombs and mind-bending substances, but Mitchell had begun to explore information focusing upon the least painful ways of committing suicide. You see, even though from the outside it looked like this kid was happily running the show in a dictatorial manner, he really had no constituency. No followers. No friends. No one liked or trusted him and he was lonely. Sure, Mitchell knew how to get attention from his mother, teachers, and the kids he held hostage by his classroom antics, but these very people had learned to avoid this rude, disrespectful, and self-absorbed young man.

Somewhere along the line something in Mitchell's game plan had gone wrong, very wrong. Because he had never learned frustration tolerance or adequate self-discipline, he tended to temper tantrum when things didn't go his way. If someone didn't seem to like him, he went into rejection mode—nailing the person first before they had a chance to hurt his feelings. In short, Mitchell had been trained to give up when challenged, to quit rather than to persevere, and to bully rather than to listen to, learn, and understand others' feelings and perceptions.

To put it bluntly, Mitchell was a mess. To be even more blunt, his mother was to blame.

Sure, we can fault his father or stepfather for their lack of involvement, but the reality was that *Cecelia was the parent in charge*, and she had long since abdicated control. Even though she complained about his behavior, no amount of nagging, hand wringing, or yakking was going to make a dent in Mitchell. This kid needed guidance, and it had to come from her, the main adult in his life. Yes, maybe it would have been different if his dad were available and had regularly disciplined the boy, but he wasn't and didn't. I couldn't turn back time, so I had to deal with the reality of a scared, intimidated mom who refused to step up to the plate and give Mitchell the discipline that he needed.

With this family there was no more time left for excuses. I went to work on Cecelia. She would have to get her act together before we could expect Mitchell to make a move. He had to believe that she would establish and support a *family code of values* that he and his brother would have to adhere to.

The code would be based upon the three basic principles of parenting.

1. Accept *discipline* as positive life guidance, not as having a negative connotation.

2. Set up *catastrophic consequences* and enforce them for negative kid actions. These must be consequences with teeth to them, not just wimpy lecturing or nagging.

3. Teach the *work ethic*, meaning you get what you earn. The entitlement ethic of *wanting* automatically leading to *getting* just wouldn't cut it anymore.

Based on these three simple but powerful principles, there were 25 Laws of Parenting that I taught to Cecelia and Mitchell over the next few months. Cecelia readily accepted some, such as the laws mandating the understanding that parent-child priorities differ and the need to squelch sibling squabbles. Other laws were more difficult for her to institute, especially setting up and following through with catastrophic consequences as well as establishing herself as a benevolent dictator. But she did learn, to her credit, to uphold most of the laws. The result? Mitchell's behavior has improved immensely and the atmosphere in the home is finally tolerable. And even though it was too late to keep David from leaving the family during the process, Cecelia rose to the occasion and continued to enforce the laws of parenting with dedication and resolve to save her family from itself.

I can't say that Mitchell was immediately thrilled with the changes in his mom or the family, but I can say he's evolved into being a much nicer young man. He admitted during my last session with him that he likes himself better now that he's not cursing at his mother or bullying his little brother. Mitchell even has a girlfriend, which I find as no coincidence. What girl in her right mind would have put up with his previous belligerent, self-absorbed, rude behavior? Sure, removing the nose ring may have helped, but I firmly believe that Mitchell's new-found self-discipline, increased frustration tolerance, and sensitivity to others were the primary reasons behind his new-found attractiveness to others.

And that's what the 25 Laws of Parenting are all about—teaching parents and others involved in the child-rearing process what really matters and what molds our children. It takes guts to say *no* to a kid who is determined to wear you down and to get his way, and it takes love to do what's right, even if the kid temporarily hates you.

You see, *discipline* doesn't mean punishment—it's the act of setting up fair, reasonable, and effective guidelines that mold children into the fine adults they soon will become. As M. Scott Peck so aptly notes in his book *The Road Less Traveled: A New Psychology of Love, Traditional Values, and Spiritual Growth*, "discipline is the basic set of

6

tools we require to solve life's problems. Without discipline we can solve nothing, and with some discipline we can solve only some problems. With total discipline we can solve all problems." Great concept, but so many parents are afraid to explore it, let alone live it. Disciplining kids takes time, which is already at a premium. It takes confidence in one's judgment as well as knowledge of child development and human nature. And it also takes *permission*—permission you give yourself to do what you know in your heart is best for your children even though that may be uncomfortable (using catastrophic consequences), time consuming (setting up a family code of values), or confusing (figuring out which parenting expert's book has the scoop on what really works).

In my own clinical practice I've seen kids who are suicidal, ill mannered, disruptive, and relentless in their pursuit of self-gratification. I've also worked with their folks, who tend to be miserable, angry, guilt-ridden, and at times suicidal themselves. These kids are tough—real tough. And their parents are getting tired of the battle.

Many of my clients have memorized the rows of parenting books littering the library shelves, and aside from becoming even more confused by the do's and don'ts proclaimed by the various experts, their child-rearing game plans are no clearer than before they turned to page one. We've been trained to view kid misbehavior from all sides—will meting out a negative consequence hurt his self-concept, will it break her spirit or set her up for adolescent risk-taking behavior? Parents have become so concerned with the effects of parenting that many resort to paralysis, inaction, or overreaction.

To fight this trend, I sorted through the case histories of the thousands of kids whom I've worked with who were either getting off track (with such problems as bratty attitudes, acting like a bully, or being painfully shy and miserable), already in trouble (such as blind followers of those involved in substance abuse), or generally out of control (using offensive backtalk, defiance of rules, and intimidation of parents, such as in Mitchell's case). From what I've learned in dealing with these families, I've been able to cull out what really seems to matter in terms of raising good kids.

That's why I wrote this book. It's here to show you that effective parenting can be simple. Mind you, I said simple, not necessarily fun. Remember Cecelia and Mitchell? They wouldn't have had a snowball's chance of change if what I asked of them was not simple, quick, and realistic.

But the 25 Laws of Parenting are easy to understand and will grow with your family. The laws give you permission to "think outside of the box" when it comes to setting up guidelines and consequences for your kids. Most folks I see, like Cecelia, are just too wimpy for their welfare or for their children's own good. They need to be given permission to parent again, to not be paralyzed by fear of damaging their children's tender egos or sensibilities, and to stand up to their tyrannical tykes. Call me old-fashioned, but somewhere along the line we've bought into the notion that kids' egos are fragile and shouldn't be challenged. That's a bunch of hooey, and, as seen in Mitchell's case, the cause of endless grief for the child as well as the parent. Heck, Mitchell is just one of many kids I know who are tougher than their folks, don't necessarily give a darn about how their behavior affects others, and are so self-absorbed that it's difficult to even get their attention, let alone squelch their spirit!

At one time or another, in their children's lives, most parents will find the need to address every single one of the concepts upon which the laws are based. If you follow my prescriptions, not only will you raise kind, responsible children, but you're bound to enjoy your family life much, much more.

These 25 Laws of Parenting have evolved over my quarter century of counseling kids and their folks and form the backbone of what I've found really matters in raising a family. Learn them, understand them, and follow them, and you will keep your family from turning into a chaotic, dysfunctional mess like Cecelia had brought upon herself.

The 25 Laws of Parenting make it clear that it's time for parents to take a stand, to draw a line in the sand, and to lay down the law. It's our job to not only provide for our children, but to guide and to protect them—at times even from their own poor judgment and lack of common sense. If you do, you will turn your kids' behavior into what you've always hoped it would be and turn you into the parent your kids deserve.

LAW #1

The Law of the Land:

Establish a Code of Values

If you believe that your kids will just *naturally* develop into good citizens or caring people, think again. Don't depend upon their peers, schools, or the media to teach them. It's up to you, their parent, to set the standards and to make absolutely clear what behaviors and character traits are important as a member of *your* family.

Kids have never been smarter than they are now. In fact, in the United States the average IQ score has risen 24 points since 1918! So this generation of kids must really have its stuff together, right? Well, on paper our children may have more smarts than we did at their age, but according to most of the research, many aren't using it. And that may not just be our problem, but our fault.

Just take a gander at today's newspaper and you'll probably read about kids involved in adult crimes or academic achievement levels falling rather than soaring. Talking with your neighbor probably won't help, as he gripes about the heathens down the road who litter his yard with their cigarette butts and empty beer cans. I'm sure that you've noticed the decline in respectful, responsible behaviors by children (perhaps yours or your friends' kids), and this surely hasn't escaped me.

But let's not rush to judge these kids. This trend falls squarely upon our shoulders—the parents of these disrespectful, impulsive kids. We're simply not teaching our children the appropriate values and respect in a way they can understand and appreciate.

Maybe, you think, it's not so bad. Their maverick attitudes are no doubt annoying, but is this really hurting the children? Well, let's see.

Take a look at what the Centers for Disease Control and Prevention found in their latest survey about the behavior of high school students.

- 70 percent admit to having used cigarettes.

- 32 percent engage in episodic heavy drinking.

- 47 percent report having used marijuana.

- 19 percent seriously considered suicide during the 12 months preceding the survey.

- 50 percent have had sexual intercourse.

Ready for some more "good" news about our brilliant offspring? Try this one on for size—the National Runaway Switchboard notes that:

- One in seven kids between the ages of 10 and 18 will run away from home.
- Assaults, illness, or suicide take the lives of 5,000 runaway youth each year.

Haven't been convinced that helping our kids to stay on track and out of trouble should be the nation's, as well as every parent's, number-one priority? Give the following a gander, taken from the National Center for Injury Prevention.

- The largest proportion of adolescent injuries is from motor vehicle crashes.
- Alcohol is involved in about 35 percent of adolescent driver fatalities.
- Alcohol is involved in about 40 percent of all adolescent drownings.

How about pregnancy?

- The United States has the highest teenage pregnancy rate of all developed countries.
- About one million teenagers become pregnant each year; 95 percent of those pregnancies are unintended and almost one-third end in abortions.

And we thought that our children were getting smarter! The reality lies in the difference between *IQ smarts* (efficiency of learning, visual and auditory memory, and perceptual-motor performance) and having developed a *good value system* (having the common sense and self-control to say no to drugs and alcohol, or the perseverance to stay in school even though the classes may be boring or seemingly irrelevant). Want to make sure that your child doesn't become one of these statistics? Of course you do, as do I as a parent myself.

Therefore, we are faced with the mission and the responsibility of setting up and teaching our children good values and acceptable societal mores.

You just can't get around it—how you raise your child matters. The values that you teach and the rules you impose have a tremendous impact not only on your kid's current behavior but also on the type of individual that he will become as an adult. Kids who are raised with a feeling of entitlement ("I want therefore I get.") or inconsistent "Teflon Rules" (slippery rules that don't stick) or wishy-washy "Velcro Values" ("I can slap the values on when I want them or just rip them off when they're inconvenient.") never quite understand or accept the laws of life. Often these children grow to be bitter, resentful adults who tend to blame others for their failures and disappointments. Until they learn to take responsibility for their actions, they will never really feel in charge of their lives and will probably be incapable of making the behavioral changes so necessary for success.

This is where establishing your own family code of values comes in.

Okay, humor me for a moment. Pretend that you were given three wishes that would guarantee the development of values and attributes that you'd like your children to possess—what would these wishes be? To have a child with perseverance and athletic talent who wows the neighborhood with his batting average or speed on a running track? How about a daughter so compassionate that she would have made Mother Teresa proud? Or, to have a kid who is so internally motivated and intellectually curious that he actually enjoys school, is enthralled with math and science, and shows promise of becoming a chemical engineer?

What attributes do you value most in yourself and others? Think about it for a moment. Do you respect honesty, reliability, and perseverance? Where do compassion, insight, and empathy fall on your list of moral priorities? And, most important, how do your children stack up in terms of these qualities? If your kid assessment is a bit spotty or even scary—join the club! I've found that many parents know what they respect in others and expect in themselves but often feel that their kids are falling short of the goal.

Why? Well, sometimes your expectations may be unreasonable or your standards too high. Kids will be kids, and it takes some life experience for feelings of compassion to kick in or to learn that honesty really is the best policy. But too often it's not from setting standards too high, but too low. Parents learn to accept bad behavior rather than taking the time to teach good values. The root of this problem is that families rarely elucidate what principles their family stands for.

The Family Code

I've found that a family without a formalized value system is like a team without a set game plan—whoever runs to first base becomes the first baseman, and the guy who meanders to the mound is the team's starting pitcher. How can you, as the team's "coach," expect to get the best out of your family that way?

And that brings us to your most important first step: Setting up a formalized code of family values. This *family code* is the recognition of the attributes, expectations, and principles that you believe to be central to the well-being of each individual member as well as to the family as a whole. Its contents are not only important but must be reasonable to attain. Not every kid can be a star athlete, but it is reasonable to expect solid participation and perseverance during practice. Your child may not become a math or chemistry whiz, but she can do all of her homework and try her best even when it's truly challenging. And your daughter may not be able at age 10 to save the world, but she can be expected to display compassion for a hurt kitten or a younger sibling who needs help.

The family code of values is a game plan of sorts. It clearly states what your family stands for as well as the behaviors that you promote. It's also "The Law of the Land," being clear about the behavior that is encouraged and the behavior you will not tolerate.

Principles such as living a substance-free lifestyle, acting in an honest and forthright manner, consistently displaying responsible behavior, and possessing a solid work ethic are some of the values in my own family code. I'm not saying that we've all achieved perfection, but we try, and the kids have grown up knowing exactly where my husband and I stand on these issues.

A bonus is that if you expect certain behaviors and value-development in your children, you have to display them yourself. Most likely you'll be a happier, more successful, and fulfilled person because of your commitment to a reasonable lifestyle.

I've found that most parents fail to set up a family code of values for two reasons—either they don't take the time to formalize the important principles that their family stands for (assuming that the kids will just "figure it out" as time goes by), or they don't want to have to follow the values and inherent behaviors themselves! Let's take a look at each of these possibilities and the associated consequences.

Excuse #1: "Let's just take one day at a time."

Many parents adopt this attitude about child rearing. It's exhausting just putting out today's fires and getting the kids off to school and to their extracurricular activities on time. Sitting down as a family to discuss something as esoteric as "values" and "expectations" may seem unnecessary, and therefore is overlooked. At times even Mom and Dad don't take the opportunity themselves to discuss such bottom-line issues as the promotion of volunteerism or whether an allowance should be earned or just given.

My clients, 18-year-old Matt and his folks, are perfect examples of "forgetting" to establish a family code of values. Sure, they had many of the bases covered, such as expecting good grades, meeting curfew, and not drinking milk directly from the carton, but they were terribly remiss in the responsibility department. Matt never quite got the hang of getting up by himself to an alarm clock (and therefore depended upon his mother to rouse him), and Dad had to constantly remind him to check to see if all of his homework was completed and packed in his book bag. Matt was a terrific kid, but one who couldn't be counted on to complete tasks or to organize his responsibilities.

Through high school Matt and his folks were able to keep things patched together haphazardly, but his dependence upon others caused major problems when he began college. Roommates are not prone to rising early just to wake up a sleepyhead, so Matt often missed his first class. Professors do not take kindly to students asking for time extensions because they forgot the paper's due date. You can see where this is going. Matt basically fell on his face, had to withdraw from his first semester, and returned home to begin at the community college to start over. This time around, though, I worked with the family, and we added responsibility to their code of values. Matt was expected to set his alarm and use a daily planner for his studies, as well as tackle other organizational duties around the house. Matt learned a hard, expensive, but ultimately very important lesson, as most of his friends were off to school and he was back home living with his folks.

Excuse #2: "But then, I'll have to change."

The second reason that many parents don't formalize and communicate a family code of values is that if they do, then *they* are expected to follow it. It's one thing to tell your kids not to smoke cigarettes or to drink alcohol, but it's quite another to live it yourself. The hypocrisy of "Do as I say but not as I do" just doesn't cut it when raising kids. You have to be willing to live the code yourself. For example, instructing your children to be fiscally responsible while you're creating a mound of credit card debt doesn't jibe.

This reminds me of a fifth-grade client of mine who had just finished the D.A.R.E. (substance-abuse education) program at school. She reported to me that on the very first day that she was planning to wear her coveted and hard-earned red D.A.R.E. T-shirt to school, she was rummaging through Mom's accessory drawer in search of a neck scarf to match. Well, the kid got more than she bargained for—underneath the scarves was Mom's marijuana stash! Not a particularly pleasant way to boast about completing a substance-abuse education course, especially when her mother had given her an "atta girl" for completing the program.

Trust me, most children know what their folks are up to, even when their parents believe that they've hidden their behavior or possessions well. Not only must you love your children enough to set up a reasonable code of values, but you must also care enough for yourself and for your family to live it yourself.

If Not You, Who?

As you can see, a family code of values is a platform upon which parents present their expectations to their kids—goals about behavior, academic achievement, truthfulness, and sexual behavior, as well as health and physical concerns. Hoping that your children "just get it" by watching you is too risky. In fact, the kids who need the most guidance in these matters are often those who are too inattentive to even notice your behavior! That's why the family code should be spelled out and communicated clearly to the kids in a formal manner, such as a family meeting. And, through the years, it should

(continued on page 20)

Creating a Family Code of Values

Here's a starter list of values and attributes you may wish to include or adapt when you set your own family's code.

In our family we value . . .

Honesty. When you tell me something, I can believe it. I can also count on you not to omit important information that you know I'd like to receive.

Perseverance. We don't give up easily. If something's tough, I expect you to keep trying. If you hit a roadblock, come to me and I'll try to help. If we can go no further, then so be it, but we give 100 percent effort.

Compassion to others. In our family we try to put ourselves in other people's shoes. I expect you to care about my and other people's feelings, and to act accordingly.

Volunteerism. When we can help others, we will. Whether this means a quick trip to deliver used clothing to the Salvation Army drop-off station or handing out sloppy joes at a homeless shelter, we will try to give back to this world some of the blessings that we have received.

Responsibility. In our household, we keep our promises and fulfill our responsibilities. If you or I say that we will do something by a certain date or time, it will be done. If we run into a problem or a time crunch, we will alert the person and work out a solution. We do not take responsibility lightly.

Zero tolerance for illegal substance use. No one in our home will use illegal substances. That includes underage alcohol usage (a substance that becomes legal at age 21) or street drugs of any kind. None, nada, zip, zilch.

Work before play. I expect you to get your homework done before going out for the evening or engaging in hours of outside play. Sure, you can take a break after school, but I don't want to deal with homework hassles at bedtime. I also expect that household chores will be performed in a timely manner. If you are employed at a job, you will be present and accounted for when required at work.

Politeness. I will be polite to you, even when irritated or annoyed, and I expect the same in return. Sure, we may get a bit testy at times, but I will apologize for my slip-ups, as I expect you to do also.

Respect for elders. Although we and your grandparents may seem a bit dotty at times and perhaps "out of it," we expect your respect. Find tolerance for our "senior moments of forgetfulness" and our old-fashioned disciplinary ways, and value our years of experience and wisdom. In return, you'll see that we will show great respect for your thoughts and behaviors.

Communication even when grumpy. When you're upset and sulky, I know that you may not want to talk with me. That's understandable. But please understand that your lack of communication leaves me guessing— I don't know whether it's something that I've done (or not done) or whether it has to do with your friends or school. Your grumpiness can frighten me and I need to know the cause. You don't have to tell me intimacies or secrets, just let me know where it's coming from and whether I can help. In return, I will respect your feelings and give you your privacy.

Athletic endeavors. We value a healthy body as well as a strong mind. Therefore, I'd like you to try out some sports, both individual and team, until you find one that you like or at least can tolerate. If not, then you need to run, jog, or exercise in some fashion at least three times a week. I'll do it with you if you want a partner in pain.

Academic achievement. In this family, we work to our potential. I don't expect you to necessarily be the straight-A student that your older brother is, but I do want you to complete all of your homework assignments and to study adequately for tests.

Reliability and promptness. I will be on time and so will you. I can be counted on to pick you up at school at 3:00 so that you are not left waiting at the back of the car line. On your part, you will be at the car line promptly so that when I drive through, you're ready and I will not hold up other parents. Also, when you say that you'll be home by 10:00, you're home by 10:00, not 10:15. When I call you in from outside play, I expect you to *hear me* and to come right home.

Sexual responsibility. I do not believe in sexual activity without a mature commitment between the partners, and that means having been together for a long time in a comfortable relationship. Usually this occurs after high school and in your college years. If you become sexually active, I expect that you will use the best protection against sexually transmitted diseases and that you and your partner will get regular checkups with your respective physicians.

be presented informally via your own actions as well as reactions to their behaviors.

If the kids tire of hearing "I expect you to tell me the truth, even if it does land you in a bit of trouble," or "We believe in work before play," so be it. This is the way that children learn what you and the family stand for. And if you're not teaching principles and values, who is? It may be your kid's peer group—now that's a scary thought! Although setting up and communicating the family code does not guarantee that the children will live by all of the principles when they become adults, some of it usually sticks. It provides them with a structure—a behavioral and attitudinal guideline to follow throughout the growing years and well into adulthood.

LIVING THE LAW

Make a list of values, attributes, qualities, and behaviors that you admire. Go for it—don't be concerned at this stage whether your ideas are totally reasonable—just get the creative juices flowing. Think about the people you admire and what it is about their behavior that you find most attractive.

Then, make a list of values, attributes, qualities, and behaviors that you definitely do not wish to see developing in your family. This list may be easier to devise—just think about folks whom you've been less than pleased with!

Together pare down both lists to those descriptors that you agree upon. If you're a single parent, then you get to do all of the choosing—definitely one of the benefits of calling the shots all by yourself. Translate, if possible, the negative attributes that you'd like to avoid into positive language. Try to keep the list to 9 or 10 items in order to keep it simple and manageable. Allow a few items to remain even though only one parent feels strongly about the attribute.

Set a family meeting to present and discuss your lists with the kids. Use firm and definitive language such as, "In our family we don't use drugs," "We're careful about using credit cards," and "We try not to give up even when it gets tough." This clarifies not only what you live by but also your expectations for the children's behavior.

As a family, periodically review the appropriateness of the values listed within your family code. As necessary, delete, add, or update the list to meet the changing needs, ages, and desires of all of the family members.

LAW #2

The Law of Discipline:

Embrace Discipline— And Use It!

Discipline is not abuse; it may not even involve punishment. If this word scares you, then you don't really understand what discipline is all about. But you better catch on quickly, since kids who are raised without it are often truly punished by society for years to come. Done well, your child will grow to be a self-confident, successful person. Done poorly, or not at all . . . well, I don't even want to go there!

L et me tell you about Natalie and Randy—these folks were a real trip! Married 13 years before the birth of their daughter Casey, they were upper middle class, highly educated and both working in the medical profession. You'd think that these people would have a clue about child rearing, but within a few minutes after meeting them I could see that it was going to be a very long therapy hour.

The way that they went on about Casey was trying my patience—it was as if the sun, moon, and stars revolved around the kid. And they expected everyone else (teachers, neighbors, friends) to view their 6-year-old with equal awe. To top that, these well-meaning parents were neurotically nervous about everything. They worried that Casey might not be able to go to a top college if her grades weren't perfect (the kid was in kindergarten at the time), fretted over whether they should have a second child so that she wouldn't feel different from her friends with siblings (I told them to get a puppy unless *they* wanted a second kid), and agonized about the potential emotional effect of even the most minute action upon their daughter's delicate psyche.

Sure, it's great when Mom and Dad love their child unconditionally, but Natalie and Randy were taking it to an extreme. They had wanted this kid for so long, suffering through three miscarriages before her birth, that they treated her as if she were some sort of miracle. Now, don't get me wrong, I marvel at how neat babies and kids can be and I also understand the agony of not being able to have a kid or two when everyone else seems to have extras. But placing a child on such a high pedestal is a recipe for disaster—not only for the kid but for the parents as well.

In Casey's situation the tragedy came in the form of not being disciplined at home. Although she turned out to be a cute, verbal young lady when I met her at our second session, Casey was somewhat of a wild child. She didn't mean to be naughty, but she seemed to have little self-control. Instead of sitting with her folks on the couch, Casey wandered the room, touching my stuff on the bookshelves and tables. I let her know that my things were off limits to her, and she'd remove her hand, only to slither back a few minutes later. Apparently *no* did not mean *no* to Casey. It meant something like "maybe," or "I'd rather you didn't," or "whatever." That's because her folks never worked on the "Do what I say when I say it" part of parenting that can be so distasteful to those who are in awe of the little miracle living under their roof. Maybe she was a miracle, but let's put it this way, the kid would have still been a miracle if given some discipline. She just would have been a more respectful, self-disciplined miracle.

Discipline Is Not Punishment

Natalie and Randy's mistake was thinking that discipline equals punishment. That's a common parental misconception, caused somewhat by the idiosyncrasies of the English language. Humor me and grab your dictionary. Look up the word *discipline* and you'll probably find the following descriptors among others: control, obedience, punishment, and regulation. Sound a bit scary, heavy-handed, or just flat out uncomfortable to you? If so, I know where you're coming from as I've heard parents, other than Natalie and Randy, lament about the need for disciplining their children and their reticence to do so. Some try to view it as analogous to a vaccine—painful to administer but certainly worth it if serious long-term problems are prevented.

Well, we're not talking about physical issues here, but mental and emotional ones. Kids need discipline—simply put—and their parents are the only ones who can teach it. Folks, you just can't pass the buck on this one, leaving it to Grandma or Grandpa, teachers, preachers, or the family down the street.

Discipline is a necessary, and possibly the most important, parental behavior that you can expose your child to. Of course, it takes self-discipline on your part to provide, and this may not be your strong suit.

24

Don't worry—if you're willing to make it through these 25 Laws of Parenting, I can teach it to you. You may feel a bit uncomfortable in the process, but hey, if Casey's folks could get it (and they did, eventually), anyone can! To get your attention, as well as your cooperation, let me send you on a guilt trip to scare you into tackling the challenge of becoming an effective disciplinarian with your kids.

Here goes. What happens if you do not raise your child with appropriate disciplinary tactics in your home? Well,

- The kid will probably grow up to be a brat.
- You'll be miserable living with a self-absorbed, difficult child.
- Your kid will never quite get the concept that the world doesn't revolve around him. The egocentricity will eventually turn off friends, dates, future spouses, and employers.
- Either your world will have to center around your child, leaving you little life of your own, or you'll get fed up and resentful about the parent/child relationship.
- As an adult, your child will not have learned to act appropriately and to accept consequences for his actions, and he'll be miserable.
- Here's the kicker: Most likely he'll blame you for his failures and misery.
- You'll be just as miserable as he is.

Discipline Is Teaching

Want to avoid this scenario? Then learn to consider discipline as a teaching process. You're the professor and your child is the student—perhaps recalcitrant but hopefully willing. And their instant buy-in isn't necessary. The laws provided in this book do not mandate your child's willing approval. Once you've begun to enforce them, you'll see how necessary and effective these simple disciplinary tactics really are.

Discipline is the structuring of expectations, the setting of limits and boundaries, and the consequences (both positive and negative) applied by parents in order to establish good frustration tolerance, perseverance, and self-discipline in your child. Learning to take "no" for an answer is a lesson in understanding boundaries. Learning to do chores even though the television is just begging to be watched or completing boring and tedious homework in a timely manner builds self-discipline. Kids who learn and live these attributes in childhood grow to be adults who can accept challenges, deal effectively with adversity, and manage relationships even when the going gets tough. They don't quit jobs because the work becomes burdensome or leave relationships because of stress and responsibility. Children who are taught discipline are not impulsive and are not quitters—they know how to deal well with, and often rise effectively to, challenges.

Discipline is a positive and loving parental action. It is the key to a happy, successful, and fulfilled life. But it is not a character trait that is inborn or innate—there are no genetic bases for self-discipline, frustration tolerance, or perseverance. These traits must be taught, and you, the parent, are your kids' best teacher. Sure, discussions at school will be helpful in molding a disciplined life, as will sermons by religious leaders and lectures by your children's coaches. But don't fall into the trap of thinking that someone else will do it all for you. Discipline is your job.

If you're a single parent, the job is placed squarely upon your shoulders. But this is often the case in two-parent households, too, when one is a bit wimpy and the other parent has to take on the role of being the chief disciplinarian. Not a comfortable position to be in, but if that's your home situation, either change it (make the other guy take some responsibility for standing up to the kids), or live with it and become the major disciplinarian yourself. Whichever way the chips fall, make sure that your children are raised in a household where discipline is key, clear limits are set, and consequences are consistent and fairly given. Not only will your life be more organized and fulfilled, but your children will grow to be successful, self-confident, and perseverant adults.

LIVING THE LAW

Ready to get going on a disciplinary plan? Consider the following:

Make it mandatory. Now that you understand how discipline is a positive term involving the teaching of consequences (both positive and negative) for behaviors and attitudes, you can embrace it as a life value—one that is imperative for your own family's happiness and success.

Clarify expectations. To ensure that all of the adults involved in the child-rearing process are on the same page of the book, clarify your conceptions of what discipline, limit setting, boundaries, and consequences are. Start with you and your spouse—your child's primary caretakers and role models. It's not unusual for parents to disagree on the battles to be picked and the wars to be fought. I've met many folks whose concerns focus upon health and hygiene, whereas their spouses' center of attention is upon grades and academic achievement. Neither is mutually exclusive—both areas have merit and should be considered in the discussion of what is really important in terms of limit-setting and expectations. Remember, though, that one of the most important relationship skills is the ability to "agree to disagree" (or, as it is in my own family—"I'll let you call the shot on this issue, but I get top billing on the next one that we can't agree upon"). That's about as fair and reasonable as you can get when two people disagree about child rearing. Note that the kids are watching how Mom and Dad resolve their differences of opinion—they are observing to see if there is effective conflict resolution going on or whether the discussion dissolves into threatening or bullying. And realize that the tactics used by parents to deal with disagreements are often the very ones that the children will try out with friends and teachers when they face differences of opinion in the future.

Enlarge the circle of influence. Don't forget to include significant others who deal with the children on a daily or weekly basis. Consider having a family meeting with Grandma, Grandpa, the nanny, and all other caregivers so that you can discuss your conception of and need for discipline in your family. These folks are looked upon by your children as role models, people to be respected and individuals to learn from. The goal of your family meeting is to consider, review, and agree upon appropriate actions to be taken when various child misbehaviors occur.

Be specific. For instance, if you want negative consequences to include timeouts and loss of privileges, then discuss these tactics with the caregivers. Where is timeout to occur? How long should it be? What is the game plan if the child leaves the timeout location early? What privileges can be removed, and are they disposed of or just put on restriction for a set amount of time? Corporal punishment can be even trickier when multiple caregivers are involved who may have disparate views on the subject. If spanking and swatting are not to be allowed, make the call, present it to the caregivers, and stick with it. Remember, your child's caregivers want to work with you but to do so successfully they need to have an adequate grasp of your disciplinary plan.

Deal effectively with disagreements. If the adults disagree on the disciplinary tactics to be employed, listen to all and discuss each issue and concern fully. You just may learn something from Grandma's more traditional values or you may end up agreeing to disagree and to do it your way. Regardless, the air will have been cleared, and there will be less chance for resentment, hard feelings, and miscommunications to occur.

Sit down with the kids. After the adults have met (in person, by phone, or even via e-mail), have a family meeting with the kids to discuss why discipline is so important in their lives, what it really means (teaching, not torture), and how it will be organized and dealt with. Listen to their concerns and make changes when appropriate. Expect some grumbling and griping—remember that kid human nature often includes pushing the limits and being a bit ornery!

Lay down the disciplinary law. Even if the kids are less than thrilled with the idea of structure, responsibility, and consequences, stick with your plan and everyone will benefit. It's not only your *right* to teach discipline, but it is also your *responsibility* as a parent.

LAW #3

The Law of Empowerment:

Don't Be a Peace-at-Any-Price Parent

Ever cave in to your kids' demands just to get them off your back or to give you a break from having to say "no" for the 110th time? Well, join the club—most of us fall into that trap every once in a while. But if you are a frequent flyer in that program, watch out! The long-term price you and your kids will pay far outweighs the temporary relief.

oday's parents are a truly heterogeneous lot—different shapes and sizes, ages, and sporting a range of marital and financial statuses. I've worked with the wealthy as well as with the financially strapped. Some have had more formal education than I, whereas others had dropped out of high school at an early age. But with all of this diversity I've found two attitudes to be universal regardless of individual differences.

- Everybody loves their kids and is trying to raise good citizens.
- Many don't have the guts to do it right.

The result is the most common mistake parents make with kids: They become a peace-at-any-price parent.

Peace-at-any-price parenting has always been around—I remember my own folks caving in once in a while, especially if I was particularly adamant and determined to get my way. The odds were in my favor if we happened to be in public and they wanted to avoid the embarrassment of disciplining a kid in front of a bunch of strangers. But they generally held their ground, the limits were clear, and I (usually) abided by their rules.

One of the best, yet saddest, examples of peace-at-any-price parenting are my clients Colleen and Gary. These are really nice folks—hard workers, yet they always find time for their three kids. Jonathan, the 16-year-old, is involved in just about any sporting activity that he can think of, and his folks generally attend his games. Gary coaches when he can, and Colleen is often found behind the concession stand hawking Cokes and hot dogs. Their 11-year-old, Brandy, excels at music—she actually plays flute in the County Youth Symphony, quite an accomplishment for a middle schooler. And then there's 6-year-old David. What can I say about little ol' Dave? Well, he certainly is active, knows what he wants, and tends to be a bit tyrannical. Where Jonathan and Brandy were fairly easygoing kids as little ones, David has always been somewhat of a pistol.

Add on that he's the baby and can be a real charmer and you can easily see that he's a kid who is used to getting his way. Over the years the family has taken to giving in to David. The family's schedule is so packed with activities that they need to be coordinated to be able to grab dinner, change clothes, and make it to the next activity without a huge obstacle getting in the way. David, however, has a chronic history of being a bump in the road. If he doesn't feel like turning off the television to go to his brother's baseball game, he has been known to throw a fit that would put a two-year-old's tantrum to shame. And David is cagey. He almost instinctively knows which games are the most important, the ones that Jonathan is anxious about and needs to arrive at early in order to effectively warm up his pitching arm. Those are the times that David digs in his heels, refuses to move, and causes such chaos that his folks and siblings either take him screaming to the car (which makes for a less than pleasurable trip) or the negotiations begin.

And that's David's plan—to get his folks over a barrel and then to go in for the kill. Colleen actually bought 10 action figures to keep on hand in order to bribe David into cooperating. If he began to tantrum and the family was in a hurry, Colleen would offer him one figure if he would just get in the car quietly so that the family could go to the game without a ton of stress. This seemed to work at first, but then David, the cagey critter that he is, upped the stakes. Realizing that once they were at the baseball field he would have another opportunity to hold his folks hostage, he would whine and fuss to go home. As Gary was usually coaching, Colleen put out the fire as best she could—by buying David candy and a soda from the concession stand.

Although these parents knew what David's tactics were, they just couldn't seem to talk sense to him. Lecturing about family responsibilities was like water off a duck's back, and no amount of appealing to his conscience seemed to work. David wanted what he wanted when he wanted it, and if he had to fuss, tantrum, or ruin the evening for his folks, that apparently was the price that he was willing to make them pay. The problem was that David wasn't paying anything for his misbehavior—in fact he was being reinforced mightily for his selfish antics.

When I told Colleen and Gary that they had evolved into peace-at-any-price parents in terms of David, they readily agreed. It just seemed to be easier to give in to his whims, desires, and demands, no matter how ridiculous they were. But David was raising the bar of bad behavior and that was concerning his folks. The previous week he had threatened to open the moving car door and jump out if they didn't turn into McDonald's and pick up some fries. That was the last straw—Colleen, who was driving, had had it with this tyrannical kid and drove straight to my office, finally willing to do whatever it took to get David's behavior under control.

First I spoke with David to make sure that the Evel Knievel stunt was just a manipulation, and he admitted that it was. He told me that he wasn't "stupid enough to jump out of a car—he just wanted the fries and a Coke." Okay, now that I was sure that he was just abusing his peace-at-any-price parents and was not really interested in hurting himself, we could make some changes in this kid and his family.

Next I brought in Gary and Colleen. I explained about the peace-at-any-price syndrome and how easy it is to fall into. But they had to claw their way out, and quickly, as David was getting way too big for his 6-year-old britches! I suggested that they have a backup plan for when he was demanding or acting out. Not only did David need to learn some frustration tolerance and self-discipline, but the daily family dramas sure weren't fair to Jonathan and Brandy. The last few years had been spent putting up with a bratty little brother, and they were beginning to become resentful and bitter toward him.

The backup plan mandated that at times one parent just

wouldn't be able to attend a function. Either Colleen or Gary had to be prepared to stay at home when David pitched a fit, in order to put him in timeout. If he started fussing in the car, he was to be warned, and if he continued to misbehave, the car was turned around, and David's butt was taken home. He would lose privileges for disruptive behavior, as well as action figures and other toys. The consequences had to hurt if his parents were to get his attention and to make him a believer. They were now willing to pay the price, and if it wasn't peaceful, so be it. I convinced them to expect up to a few weeks of tantrums and fits, but that it would be worth having a kid with self-control in the future.

I really believe that it took David pushing the family so far for these two prior peace-at-any-price parents to turn the tide. And they did. Since Gary was coaching the baseball team, he had to attend practices and games with Jonathan. So when David started in, Colleen was the one who usually stayed home with him as he was punished and sent to timeout or bed. Colleen took Brandy to symphony practice, and Gary played warden when necessary. It didn't take David long to realize that he had better straighten up his act or he would spend most of his youth in timeout. He had lost all of his action figures, and his folks were going to start giving away his PlayStation games, one by one, fit by fit, when the kid decided to call a truce.

David's self-control improved dramatically after the first few weeks, and when he began to whine, just a comment from one of his folks got his attention and he calmed down. Not only were Gary and Colleen less stressed, so were Jonathan and Brandy. Parents usually do not realize the toll it takes upon reasonable siblings when the unreasonable one rules the roost. And David was perhaps the one who benefited most from the cessation of the peace-at-any-price parenting. He gained frustration tolerance and self-discipline, and was a happier kid for it.

Give In Now, and You'll Pay and Pay and Pay

Why do such good parents as Gary and Colleen fall into the peace-at-any-price trap? I personally believe it has something to do with the stress level inherent in our hectic lives—both parents working in order to maintain chosen lifestyles and a deluge of kid extracurricular activities to attend. It just seems to be easier to give in to kids than to take a stand. What's a few dollars spent at the toy store if it magically stops your daughter's whining? Hey, isn't that a cheap price to pay for a brief respite of mental health? Or letting your son use the car on the weekend even though he's been grounded at least gets the kid out of your hair for the day, and he sure looks appreciative at the moment.

Yes, in the short term your daughter will stop whining when you make the toy store purchase or your chauffer son will flash that ol' grin that just melts your heart. But on a more basic, more important level, you've just blown it—and big time! The kids have been taught another lesson in manipulating their folks—*just whine, fuss, threaten, or nag until Mom or Dad gives in. Keep the war going until the folks call a truce, and you'll get what you wanted to begin with.* Well, if you take the bait, your children will only become more proficient at beating you down and probably will become brattier in the process.

And you'll evolve into a mental mess, wondering "Where did I go wrong?" The answer lies in the *huge* price that you inevitably pay every time that you cave in and become a doormat to your kids. Also, expect the stakes to get higher as they mature. As a teenager your daughter won't settle for a $12.00 Barbie doll—she just might throw the mother-of-all-fits at the Gap when you refuse to foot the bill for a pair of $80 jeans. And your son—that's another story. Remember how thrilled he was at 16 to be able to borrow your car on the weekend? Well, now the critter who just had his 17th birthday and is a bit too big for his own britches is demanding his own car. As he puts it, "Everyone in the senior class drives an SUV, and it's about time I did, too!" Whoa, are you getting the feeling that things are out of hand?

See how the price just went off the charts by giving in to kids for fussing when they are little? That's why it's imperative to take action *now*, before your children become materialistic monsters sporting deep-seated feelings of entitlement. Don't give in just to stop some fussing, pouting, kid grumping, or complaining. I preach to my clients that if your child isn't extremely disappointed with your lack of "giving in" or "understanding" at least a dozen times in the child-rearing years, then you've been doing something wrong!

Learn to live with the negative feelings and disappointments that they will dump on you. The emotions will subside and your children will begin to get the message that you are not a doormat to be manipulated or stepped on. You are a mom or a dad to be appreciated, listened to, and respected. Your attitude may annoy them, but you'll know that your heart and your head are in the right place.

LIVING THE LAW

Get real. Accept that you probably can't give your children 100 percent of the time, attention, and money that they would like for you to bestow upon them. Settle for giving them what *you* believe is emotionally healthy for the family, as well as for the budget.

Do not equate giving with good parenting. Sure it may work in the immediacy of the moment, but you and the child will pay big time as he grows to become more demanding and unreasonable. Giving in and becoming a peace-at-any-price parent only rewards demanding behavior and immeasurably increases the frequency of it occurring in the future.

If you don't have much of a spine, grow one. And soon. It's easy to say but difficult to do, I know. But if you start small by saying "no" to little or inconsequential requests, you'll gain self-confidence with each experience.

Turn a deaf ear. As your children see that their guilt tactics are no longer working ("But you're always at work. I need a new video game to keep me from missing you.") and are falling on deaf ears, they'll begin to get the picture, tone down their expectations, and become more reasonable.

Get in touch with how you feel as a parent. Being a peace-at-any-price parent is demeaning. I've never met a parent, in all of my years of counseling, who was comfortable with that notion and a subordinate status in the family. It comes from weakness and an inability to take a stand. Folks confide to me that they wouldn't put up with a nagging, whining employee at work, so why should they have to do so in their own home? That's baloney and intolerable! So take a stand—it's very liberating to teach them that you are not a doormat and to gain or regain their respect.

LAW #4

The Law of Authority:

Appoint Yourself Benevolent Dictator

Families are not democracies. Kid judgment can be immature, unreasonable, and self-serving. If you're not making the decisions, or are letting the kids buffalo you into doing things their way, against your better judgment, then you are depriving your kids of leadership. It's time for a new form of governance that couldn't be simpler. You have the final vote. Period. End of story.

lisa could have been the poster child for the League of Women Voters—this 7-year-old wanted everything to be fair (from her perspective) as well as to have the final vote on every family decision. As an only child, her parents, Yvonne and William, tended to dote upon her and readily admitted that the kid was a tad spoiled. A *tad* turned out to be an understatement—this child felt that the world, not only her family, revolved around her.

Alisa chose the restaurant to go to for dinner, as well as the movies to rent from the video store. She even called the shots on her mom's new car. When it came time to purchase a new one, Yvonne wanted a standard minivan, but her daughter threw such a nagging fit that the parents caved in and bought a special edition model. When Alisa described the vehicle during one of our sessions, I couldn't believe the gadgets and gizmos involved. Yvonne confirmed that they had purchased a van that was advertised on one of the cartoon networks—the car was color coded to match a certain cartoon character, and it came equipped with a built-in television and video player as well as a video game deck. The amenities of this special edition added over $2,000 to the price of the minivan but apparently Alisa's vote was final, and she was thrilled.

Needless to say, I was less than happy with a kid wielding so much power in a family. It's one thing if Mom wants the fancy car and sees value in an onboard entertainment center, but it's quite another when the child holds the parents hostage to unreasonable desires by fussing and fretting. And this wasn't an isolated event—the family had come to see me at the request of Alisa's first-grade teacher, who was concerned that the child was becoming too bossy in class as well as on the playground. The teacher was most disturbed by Alisa's constant interrupting, questions about why the class had to do certain projects and worksheets, and her tendency to cry when she didn't get her way. Thank goodness that Yvonne and William brought her for counseling—she was becoming a tyrant even before she had hit her 8th birthday!

What I taught the parents was that they had unintentionally given up the reins of power and control to their daughter. Sure, they meant well and felt that caving in was showing Alisa how much they loved and cared for her. However, the damage that was being done was tremendous. Kids need to learn boundaries and how to accept them gracefully. They should understand that their parents and teachers will listen to the kids' wants and desires, but the adults are in charge and generally get to call the final shots. Families where the child is given the final vote are usually chaotic. Children are too impulsive and inexperienced to handle that. Sure, their desires need to be heard, but the adults have the responsibility and the job of making the final decision.

Having to live within parental guidelines or learning to "take no for an answer" may not be fun, but it is imperative that this process occur during childhood. Kids raised in child-run autocracies such as Alisa's never quite learn the self-discipline necessary to get along well with others socially or on the job later as adults. Child-run families produce bratty, demanding children with parents who are held hostage to their child's next command or tantrum.

Parenting by democracy, where the child has an equal vote, only works well when the kid is mature, can view and understand others' perspectives, and is capable of planning ahead in an organized fashion. Alisa was clearly not a candidate for a democratic household. In a democracy the family members have an equal vote, and as long as they're all on the same page of the book, things seem to go along well. However, when the constituency (the kids) feel differently than do the officials (the parents), all heck can break loose. Arguing and trying to prove points take precedence over decision making, and chaos often results. When parents abdicate control to the children, when they put them on equal footing in terms of voting or veto power, no one seems to be satisfied.

Compassionate, but Still in Charge

And that's where the *benevolent dictator* style of parenting comes in. *Benevolent* means kind, caring, and compassionate, and *dictator* refers to the parent having the final vote. In a benevolent-dictatorship family all of the members have a vote (but not necessarily an equal vote), and at times the parents will yield to the kids' wishes if they are reasonable. But if a compromise cannot be reached, that's when Mom or Dad takes charge, closes the discussion, and makes the final decision. If the kids understand that this is the way that the family is run, they will accept and respect the process. Sure, there will be some grumping and "it's not fair" statements. Well, maybe it isn't always fair, but the adults have the ultimate responsibility for the safety and welfare of the children and therefore the responsibility of calling the final shots.

It took several sessions, but Yvonne, William, and Alisa were able to begin their new life as a benevolent-dictatorship family. The souped-up minivan remained, but Alisa learned to ask rather than to demand and to finally take "no" for an answer. Sure, she was not pleased with the changes in the family's power dynamics, but she grew to be a better person because of it. Not only did her parents feel more comfortable with her demeanor but so did her teacher, who reported that she was much less fussy and more of a team player at school.

Once in a while I'll see a family in therapy who has already established a benevolent dictatorship. Marcus's family was a good example of this. This 12-year-old delighted in describing his parents' crimes to me—how Mom was big on saying "because I said so" and how his father, Mario, always seemed to have the final vote on just about everything. If one were to hear only Marcus's side, it would appear that what he wanted mattered little to his parents.

However, I had the opportunity to get to know his folks intimately as I was counseling the family following the death of a grandparent. Mario, in his late thirties, came from a rather traditional Hispanic family and worked as a plumbing contractor. His wife, Suzanne, was the oldest of seven siblings, having helped her parents with the younger ones until she left for college. Her youngest brother was currently sharing their home, along with Marcus and his 9-year-old twin sisters.

Both of Marcus's parents brought a lot into their parenting that was based in their own childhood family experiences. Mario's father rarely had time to play with his three children, and he had vowed to spend more quality time with his own kids. Even though he worked long hours in his business, he still made it home for dinner and to help with the nightly bedtime ritual.

Suzanne couldn't shake her memories of "so much to do and not enough time to do it," having been responsible for helping to raise her six younger siblings. Always having been an organized person, she brought to parenting her penchant for structure. Dinner was set for 6:30, followed by baths and some family time together. Then, off to bed for the whole crew while she and Mario readied the house for the next day.

Suzanne and Mario had little trouble sticking to their schedule, and while all three kids were known to grumble and gripe about how Mom and Dad seemed to have a rule for everything, the kids generally went along with the flow. Curfews and bedtimes were adhered to even though the brood would have opted for a few more hours of TV time at night. Errand day meltdowns ("I *refuse* to go to Home Depot and the grocery store today. Mom, you should go some other time!") were unheard of. Marcus's folks believed in running their family as a benevolent dictatorship, and they were very good at it. Mario and Suzanne parented effectively and efficiently because of their commitment to taking a stand, even when it meant overriding their kids' wishes.

Benevolent-dictator parents avoid many of the hassles, disrespectful comments, and arguments that parents in family democracies or child-run autocracies tend to face. And what is even more important is that benevolent-dictator parents are not only obeyed but are respected by their kids.

Be sure, though, to remember the *benevolent* in benevolent dictator. It's important that your child feels not only loved, but respected. Listening to (but not necessarily agreeing with) your child's point of view, opinion, or argument—as long as it is presented politely—goes a long way toward proving how much you do respect your child's thoughts and opinions.

I've often used the technique that if the child is adamant about taking a stand against his folks' decision, then he can put his argument in writing. It's amazing how successful this technique has turned out to be for many of the families that I work with. For instance, if Alex sincerely believes that his 8:30 P.M. bedtime is too early and that he can handle staying up a half-hour later, then he needs to express his ideas in writing, if a short verbal discussion hasn't convinced his parents. What generally happens is that unimportant or tangential issues are often dropped when the kid has to put pencil to paper (that takes effort!). Only the truly essential issues are worth the trouble, and personally I feel that if the kid is willing to take the time to make his case in writing, then Mom and Dad need to give it special attention. Perhaps Alex *is* old enough to grab another half-hour of television before going to bed or to stay up a bit later reading a favorite book. My experience has shown me that those issues worth writing about are often significant and worthy of parental attention and perhaps compromise.

Children want limits and guidelines and are calmed by the knowledge that the parent is willing to set fair rules, employ veto power when necessary, and lead the family effectively and efficiently. Even though there will inevitably be some gripes, groans, and complaints, the end result is a more harmonious family unit.

LIVING THE LAW

Would you like to set up a benevolent dictatorship in your family? Consider the following:

Understand the difference between child-run autocracies, democratic families, and benevolent dictatorships. Each type involves a different level of parental involvement in rule making and the meting out of consequences. Think of these three parenting types as placed along a continuum of who's calling the shots—with the kids in charge in a child-run autocracy and the folks calling the shots in a benevolent dictatorship. The democratic family is in between, which requires an exquisite balance of kid self-control, maturity, and parental trust.

Take into account the ages of your children. Just as important, though, are the maturity levels of your kids—plenty of teens are less reasonable than 8-year-olds, and a family democracy mandates the usage of good kid common sense and compassion. If this isn't where your family is at this point, don't go there! Bypass the democracy and run toward the benevolent dictatorship. Finally, try not to keep up with the Joneses. Your next-door neighbors may have a higher tolerance for disrespect or misbehavior, but that doesn't mean that you have to lower your standards.

Parents, back each other up when a unilateral decision must be made. Even if all of the kids are voting in the other direction, or if you feel that their desires are either unsafe, unwarranted, or just plain too expensive, call it your way. I've often found that it's best to discuss sticky situations behind closed doors, without little ears prying into your adult conversation and decision-making process. Also, you don't need to hear tidbits of advice or opinion coming from the peanut gallery as you and your partner discuss the pros and cons of a choice. Remember: Judgment calls often reside in the gray areas of parenting. The more clear-cut issues are the easy ones to decide; it's those darn ambiguous, fuzzy decisions that mandate calm, concentrated thought and adult discussion. Don't be impulsive—take the time to "take five" and get away from the opposing attorneys (the kids) while considering your options and alternatives.

Learn to take the heat. Sure, you may not be voted Parent of the Year by your children, but you certainly will have my respect, as well as that of other parents. Raising kids is not a picnic—it can be trying and is often downright difficult. But you know what's right and wrong in your head and your heart, so follow your instincts even though you may be accused of being bossy or unfair. If your decision is in your children's best interest, it will pay off in the long run.

Don't sweat the small stuff. Let the kids have a vote when it's reasonable, and even if you disagree somewhat, let them call the shots on the little stuff. Remember, this is a *benevolent* dictatorship, not an unfair, my-way-or-the-highway style of parenting. Allowing children to feel that they have a say shows respect for their needs and desires and proves that you are willing to listen. Even if you disagree, if the consequence of your decision is negligible and the feeling of control and respect that your child gains is substantial, why not go for it? In addition, allowing your child to have a substantial voice in the minor decisions also begins her training for making larger and more significant decisions in the future. If these minor decisions are successful, she'll gain greater confidence. If not, she'll begin to realize that your input as a parent is important and worthy of her attention.

LAW #5

The Law of Cause and Effect:

Connect Consequences to Behavior

I guarantee you can get better behavior from your child. But there is only one way to do it. You must make it perfectly, unmistakably, absolutely clear that what he does will determine what happens to him. No amount of nudging, cajoling, or, worst of all, threatening, will do a lick of good until you connect consequences to his behavior.

Psychologists have long struggled with the chicken-and-egg concept of what comes first—attitudinal or behavioral change. One group believes that folks must adjust their perceptions or feelings *before* they will change their actions. The other camp campaigns for motivating behavioral change first, with changes in desires, perceptions, and feelings following.

As a behavioral psychologist I am a dyed-in-the-wool member of the latter camp. I strongly believe that changing a person's actions leads to changes in thoughts and attitudes. For example, using good study skill behaviors leads to homework completion and good grades, as well as increased knowledge in the subject. When a child is well prepared for class, it is a more enjoyable and interesting experience. Usually that results in greater class participation, even higher grades, and a heightened academic self-confidence. This in turn develops into feelings of mastery of the subject and increased interest. Voila!—a change that began as study skill *behavior* has resulted in the *attitudinal* advantage of interest and enjoyment.

Psychologists who favor a more psychoanalytic or Freudian approach would not agree with me. They believe that folks cannot change their behaviors until genuine attitudinal changes occur first. The problem with this notion, in my mind, is that I don't want to take the time to talk people into considering change. Why waste weeks, months, or even years yakking about the need to see things differently when you can motivate your children to change their inappropriate behavior within a few weeks using behavioral methods? What's more, behavioral changes lead to the development of valuable skills, such as increased frustration tolerance, self-discipline, and perseverance, that not only help your kids during childhood but will follow them into and through their adult years. In short, their future spouses, employers, and children will thank you for your diligence during this time!

I've found that the effective use of consequences and teaching what I call the "behavior-consequence connection" are the most efficient ways

47

of gaining better behavior as well as genuine changes in kid attitude. In this law and the two that follow, you'll learn the simple but effective parenting tactics that make changes fast and make changes that last.

Okay, let's try some old sayings on for size. How about, "What goes around comes around," "You get what you pay for," "You reap what you sow." All of these mean the same thing—that what you do (your *behavior*) determines what will happen to you (the *consequence*). That, in a nutshell, is the essence of the behavior-consequence connection. Try as we may to be new and innovative, those old sayings still fit. We simply cannot avoid this inevitability of human nature.

I truly believe that good things come to good people, that those who persevere and persist achieve their reasonable goals and that slackers end up bitter and resentful. Sure, some folks sneak by and get away with cheating once in a while or run a red light and avoid a ticket, but in the long run it all catches up with you. As parents, we must teach our kids that they are the masters of their destiny. Blaming others for defeats or failures is a waste of time, energy, and self-pride. Most of all, we need our children to take responsibility for their behaviors on a daily, weekly, and long-term basis.

Kids Learn Fast

Let's take a look at how this learning occurs with your child. She wasn't born with the knowledge of repercussions of behavior, but the training begins almost immediately following birth. Within a few hours your beautiful newborn started getting the hint that if she cried, she would be cuddled or fed. As a toddler she caught on pretty quickly to the idea that holding on to a table top or your hand would help keep her steady as she learned to walk. After a little more practice, she probably felt confident enough to start cruising around on her own.

As she gets older the learning continues to grow in complexity. In preschool she won't innately know that she should sit still at circle time as her teacher reads a book—she must be taught to do so. In grade school she learns about following rules by being praised for appropriate behavior (turning homework in on time) or by sitting out recess for horsing around during class.

With multiple teachers and classes to deal with in middle school, she may learn the behavior-consequence connection the hard way—by bringing home some atrocious report cards. A disorganized approach to the school day usually doesn't cut it. This means incomplete homework or being unprepared for tests. And her grades will show it. Mom and Dad are usually less than thrilled with the result and then the hammer comes down—being pulled from certain after-school activities or grounded altogether.

In high school the pressures, responsibilities, and dangers grow. With driving and curfews come rules that she may choose to obey or disregard, with drastic consequences. As a teen she'll meet kids with all types of values (ranging from horrific to terrific), and she must make behavioral choices as to whether to engage in substance use, sexual activity, or slacking off academically. I've worked with many teens over the years who ignore or flat-out deny that their behavior has real consequences, or they admit it but resent the adults who remind them, and attempt to make their lives miserable as a result.

I've also met many kids who are rarely allowed to feel the repercussions of what they do. Mom or Dad may "fix" the problem for the kid (repair a damaged car without the teen pitching in with some of his own money), defend the child inappropriately ("My Tommy would never come up with the idea of sneaking out at night. Your Johnny must have pressured him into it!"), or ignore the behavior altogether (not checking or commenting upon poor report cards). Although well-meaning, folks who do not allow their children to be held accountable for their inappropriate behavior actually deprive them of learning the behavior-consequence connection and perpetuate the myth that whatever they do is okay.

One of the best examples of a thickheaded kid not being trained to respect the behavior-consequence connection was Chance—a real cutie whom I first met when he was 12 years old. His mom brought him to see me because he was about to be booted out of his private-school classroom for acting up as well as failing to complete homework or to study for tests. During class, Chance was hysterical—he could break up the class with his stand-up comedy at a moment's notice, and he was usually game for some impulsive risk-taking, especially if it involved entertaining the troops by making rather gross body function noises. The interesting thing was that although he spent more time fooling around than paying attention, Chance consistently made great grades, report card after report card. His parents weren't concerned that he displayed few, if any, study skills, and they thought that his antics were actually amusing.

After interviewing Chance, though, I found little humor in his irresponsible attitude toward his studies as well as his behavior toward his classmates and teachers. At 12 years of age and in the sixth grade, this intellectually gifted child was able to get by academically by depending upon his excellent memory and terrific verbal skills. He had a knack for eliminating incorrect answers to multiple-choice questions and could produce an essay with ease. That is, in the sixth grade. I cautioned this young man that his intellectual and high-level reasoning prowess would take him only so far, and that in the not-too-distant future his lack of organization, planning, and study skills would catch up with him. Well, Chance was not buying into my predictive abilities, and since his folks didn't seem to care whether he did his math homework or not (as long as the grade on the report card was acceptable), he chose to continue his irresponsible ways. By the end of the school year, the administration had had it with him, and his admission contract was not renewed. So, off to public school he went.

I next caught wind of Chance in his senior year in high school. Although no longer quite the cutup of his middle-school years, he still did not see the need to do things that were not particularly interesting or fun.

His homework was sloppy, if completed at all, and he continued to rely on his intellect to get him through his classes. But it was no longer working—Chance was learning the hard way that without the proper behavior (studying), negative consequences would occur (a poor grade point average and low SAT scores). His parents brought him to see me at that time because Chance was becoming depressed. Most of his friends were headed to 4-year universities in the fall, yet Chance had not been accepted at any of his choices. He would have to do his time at the local community college, and if he got his act together and made good grades, perhaps he would be able to hook up with his buddies for his junior year in college. At 17 years old, Chance was finally getting the message and was beginning to regret his irresponsible ways. But he was going to have to pay the price and bear the consequences of his previous actions.

Think your child is just going to pick this up on her own? Willing to bet her lifelong happiness on it? That's really what you're doing if you're not actively involved in teaching this lesson. Sure, she'll run into some consequences with teachers and friends along the way, but there are so many more teachable moments available to you at home and during family activities. She doesn't have to learn through pain. It can be done in a normal, everyday fashion—without the dreaded sit-down formal lecture.

For instance:

- When your little one grabs her favorite cereal box off the shelf at the grocery store (behavior), say "no" and have her replace the box on the shelf (consequence) and move on. If she asks politely and it's a reasonable request (behavior), say "yes" and have her put the cereal into the shopping cart (consequence).

- When your grade-schooler "forgets" about some homework until bedtime (behavior), set the alarm clock for 30 minutes earlier the next morning (consequence) so that she can get it done before school.

- If your middle schooler leaves her lunch money at home (be-havior), don't deliver it to her. She can either go hungry that day or mooch some food or cash from her friends (consequence).
- Your heavy-footed (behavior) 17-year-old can pay for her own speeding ticket or attend Saturday driving school for a few weeks (consequence) rather than you taking care of the bill for her.

The faster that kids learn the connection between what they do and the effect that it has upon others, the faster they begin to under-stand the idea of responsibility and outcome. They tend to think be-fore acting, are less impulsive than their peers, and are often socially and academically successful. In addition, home life is much more com-fortable as you find yourself having to nag and remind less, activities not only frustrating to you but very annoying to your child.

Moreover, the ultimate goal of guiding your child into a self-disciplined adult is achieved. Kids who are allowed and encouraged to learn the behavior-consequence connection evolve gracefully into responsible adults. Extra chores or obligations are handled appropri-ately and challenges are seen as just that—something to be accom-plished, not problems to be avoided.

LIVING THE LAW

It's never too soon or too late. Realizing that brand-new babies begin to make the connection between what they do and what they get should solidify the idea that your 13-year-old daughter can understand the concept also. Don't give up on her—even if she professes to "forget" or to "just not get it," don't buy into that. She'll figure it out quickly if there is something in it for her—be it positive or negative.

Take advantage of teachable moments. Although you don't need to go on and on about the behavior-consequence connection, if you see an opportunity (and there's probably at least one each day), bring it to your child's attention. Now, that doesn't mean that you're constantly criticizing the kid. You're just teaching her that making fun of her friend may lead to retaliation or at least a lessened friendship, or that getting a speeding ticket on her record will mean higher insurance premiums for years to come.

Watch out for feelings of entitlement. Be careful that your children do not take everything for granted—make them work for their allowances and privileges so that they see that effort leads to results! If they complain that it's unfair that they have to work more than their friends, call a family meeting to discuss why you are making such a fuss about the behavior-consequence connection and why living it is so important to your family.

Check your own behavior. It's really not a good idea to run a red light or to do one of those "rolling stops" at the stop sign. Even if you don't get a ticket from a policeman, your kids may believe that there are two sets of rules out there—one for your family and one for the rest of the world. Remember, they are watching how you follow the rules and will most likely behave in a similar manner as they grow.

Don't assume anything! Presuming that your kids will understand the connection just by attending school or playing with the neighborhood children is risky business. You may get lucky and have a mom or dad down the street who points out the behavior-consequence connection to your kid, but most will not. Folks tend to be reticent about disciplining other people's children. So if you hear that your child acted up at a friend's house or misbehaved in school, do something about it yourself. Sure, it may be double jeopardy, but I'd rather have the idea securely instilled in your kid than take the chance of it not becoming part of her personal value system.

LAW #6

The Law of Structure:

Establish Daily Expectations

Tried *everything* to get your kids to do as they're told when told or to take "no" for an answer without griping and groaning? Do you want them to make their beds, feed the dog, and get their homework completed on time, accurately, and without a hassle? Well, just follow this easy plan. All it takes is clear and meaningful consequences!

By the time that most families land in my office, they've tried just about everything to get their kids' behavior under control. Some swat and smack, others coax and reason, and many have tried parenting programs that they read about or learned about on television. Almost any tactic will get kids' immediate attention, but most children quickly lose interest and return to their noncompliant, rude, or otherwise inappropriate behavior. And most folks give up when their children no longer respond. Maybe the parents will go on to try other parenting techniques or, once they get pooped out, just throw in the towel for a year or two and hope for the best.

In my experience, checking out for a few years only ends up with kids who are more problematic, so that's not a route I suggest. What I would like you to consider, though, is using my behavior management system—one that I developed over 25 years ago and have used and improved upon throughout that time. All families need structure, rules, and expectations spelled out for their children, and that's exactly what my program does. In my previous books *Don't Be Afraid to Discipline* and *It's Never Too Soon to Discipline*, I describe in detail how to set up behavior management programs for preschoolers, grade-schoolers, tweens, and teens. Charts are provided and the methodology is presented in great detail. But to get you started with an effective yet simple management system, my Law of Structure gets to the gist of what you need to set up a program that will work for your family.

The Law of Structure is based on four action items.

1. Develop a list of expectations or chores.

2. Establish what behaviors or attitudes are acceptable and which ones have to stop.

3. Link *behaviors* (expectations and attitudes) with *consequences* (the behavior-consequence connection) and establish the rules for having a *Good Day*.

55

4. Provide the consequences in a consistent yet nonchalant fashion.

Step One: Develop the Lists

Ready to set up the system for your own family? You'll need to create two lists.

First, consider what chores and expectations you have (or want to develop) for your children. These can include activities to be completed before school (make bed, brush teeth, feed the dog), after school (complete homework, take out the trash), and following dinner (family room pickup, clean up bedroom, shower, and clean up bathroom). Kids don't need a ton of chores, so try to focus on jobs that are important to daily functioning. On weekends the chores or expectations may be lessened or different—just be reasonable. This makes up the *expectation list*—the chores that we want our kids to complete each day.

The second list contains the pesky attitudinal or behavioral issues that all kids exhibit at one time or another in their development: talking back, not taking "no" for an answer, not doing as they're told, interrupting, leaving without permission, fighting with and teasing siblings, whining, fussing, crying, and so on. These behaviors merit what I call *bad points*—the stuff we want to keep down to a dull roar.

Step Two: Communicate What Is Acceptable—And Keep Score

Now it's time to determine how much goofing off or problematic attitude is allowed each day before your child loses her daily rewards. Since no one is perfect, you have to expect some minor misbehavior or rudeness from kids. Notice that I said minor—anything major needs to be addressed, but we can let some of the little stuff go.

I suggest allowing two expectations a day to go unfulfilled if the total number of chores is seven or more. If your chore list contains five or fewer, then perhaps allowing only one to slide is appropriate. Keep in mind that to get credit for chore completion, the child must do it without a hassle (no whining, fussing, or crying), on time (by a certain time of day, or better yet, beating a buzzer that you have set in order to better motivate task completion), and correctly (homework done well or dirty clothes put in the hamper and not shoved under the bed). Only if these three criteria are met does the child get credit for completing the expectation that day.

Then, set a limit for the number of attitudinal/behavior bad points that are allowed each day. Generally, I'll begin a program allowing eight bad points per day—this may seem like a lot, but it really isn't if you're nailing your kid for rude remarks, bugging his sister, or yelling instead of talking. Trust me, bad points come quickly once you have the guts to give them out.

Okay, so we're setting the rule that the kid needs all but two of his chores completed and no more than eight bad points in order to have a Good Day. Once you get this down, it's easy to keep track, especially if you've drawn up a weekly chart, placed it on the refrigerator, and are marking it consistently. You'll see especially cagey kids checking it out throughout the day—making sure that they use up every bad point that they are allowed but still staying within the criteria for having a Good Day. No problem with this manipulatory gesture. It just shows you've succeeded in getting their attention! When you lower the number of bad points allowed as time goes by, their behavior will adjust to meet your higher standards.

Step Three: Make the Connection

Now it's time to link the behavior with the consequences. I've found that kids respond best to earning tangible rewards they can accumulate and use. The most success I've seen has been with a system that uses five kinds of rewards and works like this:

- A red poker chip to be used as money for allowance purchases (for grade-schoolers and older)
- A blue poker chip worth a set amount for clothing (for tweens and teens) or for special toys or video games (for younger kids)
- A white poker chip that can be saved up to turn in for special privileges (going to the movies, a favorite restaurant, concerts)
- Use of electricity (using anything that either uses batteries or plugs into the wall—telephone, television, computer, Game Boy), and
- Playtime/freedom (going outside to play or swim for younger kids and using the car, sleepovers, and so on for teens).

The three poker chips, electricity, and playtime/freedom are given as rewards when the child has earned a Good Day or are lost if a Good Day is not achieved. I've learned that to make a dent in a kid's behavior, you have to first get their attention, and these consequences usually do.

If you have a child who is especially ornery or stubborn, you may need to raise the consequence bar—in terms of rewards as well as punishments. That's where Law #7, The Law of Being Heard, comes in. Check out that law next even if your child is reasonably compliant—someday those ideas just might come in handy!

Be sure to follow through on your end of the bargain, whichever way it goes. If the child earns a Good Day, give her the three poker chips (red, blue, and white) as well as allowing reasonable electricity use and playtime/freedom. If your daughter doesn't earn the Good Day, either by not completing most of her chores or by displaying a negative attitude and accumulating too many bad points that day, she receives no poker chips, and all electricity (except essentials like lights, blow dryers, and alarm clocks) and playtime/freedom are suspended until the next morning. The kid will certainly gripe about the negative consequences, but remind her that tomorrow is another day, and she can work to regain her rewards then.

Step Four: Be Consistent

I can't tell you how many folks will set up my program and come back to see me 2 weeks later with great-looking charts. Many are thrilled with the results, the system keeps both the kids and their folks accountable, and that's why it works. However, some families return with behavior charts that look terrific, but when I question the parents about how it's going, I'll hear responses such as, "He nags and nags me after I say no" or "I still have to remind her five times to clean her room!" Obviously these folks are not using the system—they are either afraid to give out bad points because it will anger their children, or they are just too lazy to get up and mark them on the chart. Many children report that their parents will threaten big-time but do not follow up with a bad point no matter how ill-behaved they are. Now I understand folks who don't want to anger their kids or are too lazy to get their butts off the couch to mark the chart. But what I have trouble comprehending is why they continue to see me in private practice, paying a lot of money to get my ideas and advice and then not heeding it!

When I bring this enigma to their attention, the parents usually admit that they've slacked off and vow to do a better job over the next few weeks. I'm sure that my blunt demeanor scares a few families off, but most continue and are embarrassed into being consistent with the consequences and complying with my program. And those families do reap the benefits—kids who are more compliant, parents who nag less, and a genuinely pleasant atmosphere in the home. Believe me, if they can do it, so can you—just follow and live the law.

LIVING THE LAW

Call a family meeting. Before presenting the program to the children, however, Mom and Dad need to decide upon assigned chores and expectations and which behaviors or attitudes they wish to work on with each of the kids. Often, the majority of points will be the same for all of the kids, with some idiosyncratic issues to be dealt with for each child. Try to agree or compromise on what's important.

Let the little stuff go. Stick with the important behaviors and daily expectations. If you make your list or chart too long or complicated, most likely you won't complete it—and the kids will notice and begin to slack off.

Present the program. At the family meeting describe the idea of a behavior management program to the children. Don't focus on or blame one particular kid—state that it's a system to help *everyone* get along better. Let them know that this will help prevent you from nagging and complaining about their behavior and that they can earn some great privileges by following the system. Buy the necessities. Purchase a few kitchen timers, perhaps one for each family member. Explain how you will use it—setting the timer for 10 minutes for bedroom cleanup, 5 minutes to get dressed in the morning, and 15 to take a shower and wipe up the puddles. Confirm that not beating the buzzer will result in a bad point. Also, purchase the poker chips to use in exchange for allowance money, clothing funds, and special privilege points.

Set up the system. Review what chores and expectations each child must accomplish successfully each day and how many can be missed and still achieve a Good Day. Go over the bad points section of the system, clearly stating what will constitute a bad point and stating how many each child can accumulate each day and still receive their rewards. Go over the consequences that they will receive or lose, depending upon work effort and behavior/attitude during the day. Make a list of what privileges can be "bought" with the white poker chips and how all of the chips can be cashed in.

Answer any and all questions, even the small stuff. The better prepared you and the kids are for the system, the more successful it will be. Clarify ambiguities and gray areas, explain miscommunications, and describe why certain behaviors will be counted as bad points.

Compromise when appropriate, but stick to your guns if the behavior in question is important to your family code of values.

Be nonchalant. If you have to give negative consequences, watch that you are calm and not yelling. Nothing gets a kid's attention like a quiet parent patiently removing privileges. Many children are so used to screaming parents that it's either water off a duck's back, or you've just handed them reason to really be annoyed or angry with you. Give the consequence and move on.

Live the system. Set a start date and get going on the system. The first few days may seem a bit tedious in terms of marking the chart, but after you and the kids get the gist, it becomes second nature!

LAW #7

The Law of Being Heard:

Make Consequences Catastrophic

If your child is especially irritable, defiant, or just plain lazy, then you need to raise the bar on the consequences that you use to motivate behavior. If it doesn't "hurt," then it won't work. To get the kid's attention (and compliance), you have to think outside of the box—get creative and get catastrophic! Their turnaround will be nothing short of miraculous. I can't begin to tell you how many times in my career, or for that matter how many times in just a week, I hear a parent say, "Nothing seems to affect my child. Timeouts don't work and taking away privileges is a waste of time. My kid is immune to consequences!" I try hard to keep it in, but my response is always the same: "Uh-oh, here we go again."

like to refer to this parental attitude as *having a case of the wimps*. Most of my parent-clients just don't get it—they believe that a few minutes in bedroom timeout or loss of evening television time should make a dent in their child's behavior. Wake up, Mom! Many kids are way too ornery to be affected by hanging around in their bedroom for 5 or 10 minutes. Even losing the bike for an afternoon or a week can be dealt with. No bike? I'll just go on the computer. No computer? I'll just talk on the phone or watch videos or paint or—well, you get the picture. There's so much else to do that such a wimpy timeout or privilege loss is like water off a duck's back.

Take Marnie, for instance. This cagey 11-year-old had her parents' number down pat. When she would leave the house without permission, talk back too much, or get too ornery, her folks would send her to her room. Marnie confided to me that she really didn't mind it. Her bedroom was full of things to do—she'd write in her journal, finish some homework, or listen to CDs. No big deal—she could handle it fine! No wonder the kid continued to be noncompliant and sassy to her folks—their consequences were of no consequence to her.

When I met with Mitzi and Jim, Marnie's parents, my job was to teach them that consequences for inappropriate behaviors had to be *clear, catastrophic,* and *consistent.* The clear and consistent parts seemed to have already been memorized from reading various parenting magazines and books, but the catastrophic philosophy was a new one to her folks. Their first question was, "Does that mean we have to spank Marnie?" Great question, and one with a simple answer: Probably not. It's not that I'm dead set against it in all cases, but the reality is that spanking is generally ineffective. Most of my families find other consequences to be longer lasting and something that they can better tolerate.

Relieved that they weren't going to be instructed to beat the tar out of their daughter, they listened as I proceeded to describe what cat-astrophic consequences really are. The bottom line is that the action must hurt by either "hitting" the kid in the pocketbook or wallet or by boring her to tears. Kid human nature is very simple. One of the main tenets is "I'm not gonna listen unless it affects me." That's why reasoning usually doesn't work, nagging and repeating are efforts in futility, and short timeouts are really just a waste of time. To affect a kid it has to really get their attention.

I asked the family to consider the following scenario. Every time that Marnie had to be asked or reminded to do the same thing three times in a row, Mitzi or Jim would take one of her possessions away and give it to a homeless shelter or the Salvation Army. No, it wasn't going to be "saved" in her parents' closet to be returned or earned back at a later date. The possession was history—gone, out of there. Marnie could save up her money and buy another CD, ring, or board game, but that would be her decision and her re-sponsibility.

You should have seen the kid's jaw drop when I laid down the law—she could barely get out, "But that's not fair, that's my stuff and they can't just take it away!" That's absolutely true—it was her stuff, and Mom and Dad would now be told, by Marnie's inappropriate ac-tions, to get rid of it, not "just take it away." Mom and Dad would just be keeping score, but it would be Marnie's behavior that would deter-mine what happened.

I offered the family another way to make the consequences cat-astrophic—lengthen the timeout period to at least 15 minutes with the option to raise it significantly if a shorter time period didn't seem to get Marnie's attention (and more appropriate behavior). And I threw in that we'd be changing the timeout location to a dif-ferent, more boring spot than her bedroom. I suggested using a bathroom (only after it had been kid-proofed and was absolutely safe and completely boring), a guestroom, or a hall with a baby gate installed in the doorway. Sure, Marnie could remove the gate and leave timeout, but then a possession would be taken and given away. At this time in the conversation I have to admit that I was certainly not making many points with the kid, but her folks were beginning to get my message. *If you want to tone down inappropriate behavior, to get your kid's attention, and to increase the respect level in your home, catastrophic consequences must be employed, especially with ornery kids.*

I saw the family again about 2 weeks after our initial meeting, and boy, had things changed. Marnie had lost three Beanie Babies and an NSync CD during the first week of using the new law. After that, though, she seemed to have gained the self-control to do what she was asked by the first or second request. Her parents were shocked that this law had worked so well in such a short time. I wasn't, as I have seen the exact same exquisite result of catastrophic, clear, and consistent consequences countless times for almost a quarter of a century in my psychology practice.

Interesting and wonderful things happen as parents begin to take control of their children's inappropriate behavior by employing catastrophic consequences. The folks feel better about themselves as parents. They are no longer nagging and yelling or cajoling an unmotivated and nonresponsive kid. The child miraculously seems to have more energy. Kids quickly get off the couch to brush their teeth or to clean up the pile of Legos sitting in the middle of the family room floor. Their hearing also improves significantly. No longer will parents have to listen to, "But I didn't hear you" once kids start losing possessions or suffering through lengthy timeouts at the third request. Just chalk this miracle up to a newfound understanding of kid human nature and working with it, not in ignorance of it.

LIVING THE LAW

Wondering how to make consequences more catastrophic? Well, this is how I begin with my own clients during therapy.

Think about what your kid loves to own. What does he collect (Beanie Babies, baseball cards, toys from McDonald's Happy Meals), buy (CDs, football jerseys, video tapes), play with (Lego sets, actions figures, Barbies), or wear (Gap shirts and jeans, shoes, shoes, and more shoes, T-shirts with slogans)? Consider these as prime possessions to take away and to give to a homeless shelter. Some needy child will certainly appreciate the donation and your kid will most likely miss owning the items.

Consider what your child loves to do. Watch television, IM buddies on the Internet, go outside to play or swim in the pool, or talk on the telephone. Taking away all of these privileges for the rest of the day or for the next 24 hours, alone or in addition to giving away a possession, should get your kid's attention and motivate better behavior.

Think about what your child doesn't like to do. Weed the garden, clean out the garage, wash windows, or clean the cars. These are great catastrophic consequences that can be meted out whenever bad behavior occurs, and the child has to complete the chore that day or that weekend. Keep it reasonable, though—expecting your son to mow the lawn in the dark is dangerous and inappropriate. Pick another, more practical chore to assign that night.

Check out alternative timeout situations. A bathroom or boring guestroom timeout for an extended period of time works wonders. Take your child's age into consideration, and then double or triple the time period that you normally would assign. For example, 5-year-olds can sit in timeout for 30, 45, or 60 minutes. A particularly stubborn 10-year-old may have to pull 2 to 3 hours of timeout before it begins to make a dent. Use your judgment as well as your schedule to determine what would work best.

Set up the if/then rule, with a behavior and a consequence.
Some behaviors might include, "If I have to ask you more than twice
to do something," or "If you talk back more than three times in a day,"
or "If you perform any physical violence" (hitting sibling, slamming
doors, hurting a pet). Some consequences include, "then you will end
up in timeout," or "then you will lose a possession or be assigned an
additional chore."

Call a family meeting. Explain the new rule, how it works, and
put it into action. Then, sit back and watch the kids actually move
when you make a request!

LAW #8

The Law of Abstinence:

Have Zero Tolerance for Substance Use

Any substance *use* (drugs and/or alcohol) is substance *abuse*. No ifs, ands, or buts about it. It's illegal, dangerous, addictive, and has absolutely no place in your family. Learn the signs and symptoms of use and how to keep your children substance free. If you don't take a stand, how can they?

Notice that the title of this law is "have zero tolerance for substance use," not abuse. What's up with this? Well, after years of working with kids who get involved in smoking, swallowing, huffing, injecting, and snorting anything that they can get into, I've come to the conclusion that kid substance use is synonymous with kid substance abuse. Even though they may try to convince you otherwise, these young critters just don't know when to call it quits, before it's too late. I know, I know, when we were kids and could get our hands on some beer to drink or cigarettes to smoke, many of us indulged. But it just seemed different back then, and not only because it was our generation doing it. It really was different. Yes, cigarettes were easy to obtain—you could often buy them from a vending machine when an adult wasn't looking. And sure, a dedicated lush could scrounge up a six pack in high school or a keg in college, but that took some planning, money, and plenty of moxie. Today, the drugs that our kids are exposed to are more toxic and addictive. Kids tell me about alcohol and drugs brought to school, stashed in book bags, pockets, or sneakers. I have several clients who smoke marijuana on an almost daily basis—they go to school stoned, sleep through many of their classes, and do a crash and burn in the afternoon, telling Mom that they're tired from classes and need to take a nap.

And then there are the even scarier risk seekers, those who are looking for the latest in designer drugs—mostly pills, but also inhalants and liquids. These kids, knowingly or unintentionally, are risking brain damage through organic toxicity as well as disruption to their daily routines, schools, safety, and families.

Substance abuse counselors often view drug or alcohol dependency as falling within four progressive stages of development or severity.

1. *Initial usage* involves a minimal number of episodes (about five or less) and the usage hasn't yet interfered significantly with daily functioning. The child still attends and participates

in classes, is engaged in regular extracurricular activities, friendships, and family relationships. The tween or teen may view the substance as a way to gain acceptance into a social group, to alter feelings, or to deal with discomfort.

2. *Problem usage* involves using the substance on a more frequent basis. In addition, the child's thought process moves from perceiving substance use as "a possible way of" to "the best way of" altering negative feelings or being accepted by others.

3. *Psychological addiction* is stage three. At this level the youngster is often very open about his drug usage and quite defiant about others' attempts to help or to stop it. Kids begin to look forward to binges, to depend upon the "good" (although temporary) feelings associated with substance use, and often show an increased tolerance for their drug or alcohol of choice.

4. The most severe stage, that of *physiological addiction*, contains all of the symptoms and signs of stage three but the body chemistry has adapted to the drugs taken. Therefore, detoxification procedures must be cautiously implemented if physiological withdrawal is to occur.

Liquor is often the substance of choice for many of our young people. Although illegal to sell to anyone under the age of 21, a determined teen can usually find a way to secure some booze. Kids raid their parents' liquor cabinets (lock 'em up, folks!), pay an adult to buy it from the local convenience or liquor store, or use false identification to buy from a store themselves. Beer, wine, and hard liquor can become addictive, and alcoholism is one of the top health as well as mental health problems in our culture. Alcohol addiction often leads to loss of motivation, DUIs, and other illegal involvement. Safety can be compromised, as are judgment and self-control. The disinhibiting effect of alcohol may feel good, but the behaviors and consequences that follow are a large price to pay for continued usage. Psychological and physiological dependency follow, and detoxification procedures may be necessary.

In addition to liquor and marijuana, it's important for parents to become aware of other drugs of choice of our kids. The following is a primer of some of the more common substances used.

Ecstasy (MDMA). This is a widely available drug (in pill form) often known as the "happy pill" as it makes people excited and euphoric. However, ecstasy may cause permanent brain damage by killing cells that release the neurotransmitter substance, serotonin. Side effects can include increased heart rate, possible stroke or heart attack, seizure, or dehydration.

Nitrous oxide (whipits). This is a favorite of the middle school set—mainly because it is easily obtained and "legal." Nitrous oxide is a gas that is used in some aerosol sprays, such as cans of whipped cream and other foodstuffs. Dealers also sell it in balloons. The effects that it can have on the user are very similar to alcohol intoxication. Seizures or permanent brain damage can be caused by the depletion of oxygen to the brain.

Dextromethorphan (DXM). Another favorite of the younger group as it is legally and readily available. This liquid is taken orally and is found in many cough suppressants, such as Robitussin. If taken in high doses, it can be a hallucinogen and cause coma or suppress breathing.

Crystal methamphetamine (crank). This stimulant can be smoked, eaten, snorted up the nose, or injected in a vein. It causes the user to feel happy, increases energy, and can result in psychotic behavior.

Heroin. This narcotic is highly addictive. Heroin is a relaxant and can cause a dangerously slow rate of breathing. This substance is used by injection, snorting, or smoking.

With all of the drugs available and their potential side effects, you would think that parents are on top of their child's substance use. Sadly, though, many are not. Kids can be so sneaky that often substance use has to become a distinct problem before parents notice. Consider Chas, for instance. This kid was 14 years old, a decent student and part-time athlete. On paper he looked good—went to school most days, although he rarely seemed to have homework to do, was present and accounted for at the dinner table, and dressed in a preppy manner. The bad news was that Chas was a pothead. The kid could smoke two to three joints a day, every day, and still function, although at a decreased level. His grades had dropped since beginning high school, and his hustle at football was marginal. Chas just seemed mellow—not argumentative as his folks Charles and Nancy thought a druggie would be. You can imagine how surprised they were when their kid's urine screen for his high school physical came back positive for cannabis (marijuana) as well as nicotine. The boy had been smoking dope and cigarettes for over 4 months without his parents suspecting anything.

Well, once Chas was nailed, his folks brought him to my office at his pediatrician's suggestion. He knew that the gig was up, and although he personally saw nothing wrong with smoking dope on a daily basis, he did admit that it probably was not such a hot idea since it freaked out his parents. He also acknowledged that his motivation for academics and athletics had decreased over the months and that he had to make some changes if he wanted to go to college.

Since he was already in such hot water, Chas told me of his frequent alcohol use—mostly beer when he could get it. He noted that he preferred marijuana to liquor—it was easier to get and more difficult for his parents to detect. In order to work on Chas's addictions, he needed to stop using, and to do so immediately. I told the family that no substance use should be tolerated—I don't believe in "social" or "recreational" use of substances for kids. You either say "no" to all drugs and alcohol or run the risk of the recreational user becoming a frequent flyer.

Because he had been dishonest and sneaky (swiping liquor from his folks' cabinet, smoking a joint on the walk to school), I instructed the family to avoid trust situations for the present. That meant that they were not to take Chas's word that he was abstinent—he had too great a history of lying and sneaking, and most likely would revert to that if given the chance. We had to go in for the kill to help motivate him to stop using, and I suggested employing regular urine drug screens as well as alcohol tests. The drug screens were given at the pediatrician's lab, and Chas went every 2 to 3 weeks. His parents bought an Alco-Screen product from the local pharmacy to keep his drinking behavior in check.

Almost immediately these measures were successful. Once Chas knew for sure that his folks would be administering these screening devices, he was smart enough to knock off the drug and alcohol usage. His parents also paid closer attention to his whereabouts and the people that he was hanging out with, and his free time was initially restricted to supervised activities. Because Chas knew that he would be caught red-handed, he stopped using. The screening measures gave him the motivation to no longer use substances as well as a convenient excuse to use with his friends when they tried to pressure him into partying.

Well, I've worked with Chas for over 2 years now, and he continues to stay clean and sober. I have little doubt, though, that had we screened for only a few months, Chas would have returned to his druggie behavior and usage. That stuff is so addictive that it not only becomes a psychological habit but can also result in physiological addiction. The most important motivator was his fear of getting caught using, with the consequence being sent to a drug rehabilitation center. This reaction to drug and alcohol screens is not unusual for tweens and teens. Most will stop using substances if they believe two things: That their folks will really pay for, and take the time to arrange for, the drug screens, and that if the reading comes out positive, then a tour of duty at a drug rehab is in order.

73

A couple of years ago I was involved as an expert on *The Oprah Winfrey Show* on a program entitled "I Was a Parent in Denial." It was a great hour, but the most important point, in my opinion, was that *every one* of the teens on the show admitted that had their folks employed drug screens, especially early in their substance abuse careers, they would have stopped using out of fear of getting caught and the consequences they would have had to face. Pretty powerful stuff those screening devices, and I highly recommend them to parents who have reason to believe that their child is using. Now, I wouldn't drag every kid into the laboratory and have them pee in a bottle just because the technique works—only kids who have "drawn first blood." That is, they have shown signs and symptoms of substance use, and you are suspicious of what they are into. It's insulting for a straight kid to be accused of using, so please be fair in your assessment and your behavior.

LIVING THE LAW

Talk to your kids about substance use and abuse. Studies have shown that parents who hold conversations (notice the plural, not just one quick lecture on the way to the ballpark) about the pitfalls of drug and alcohol use help to prevent addiction in their children. In your own discussions with the kids, give examples of people they know who have faced difficult consequences because of substances, such as dropping out of school, poor health, divorce, loss of job, and family upheaval.

Discuss media and peer pressure. Your children are besieged with images, both visual and auditory, about how cool it may be to use drugs, alcohol, or cigarettes. To combat this, supervise their TV viewing and music choices, and discuss how peers may pressure your children to engage in substance use. Promote a home environment that allows for and invites communication on this topic.

Be a good role model. Don't do drugs yourself. I don't care that it's "only marijuana"—it's illegal, addictive, and a lousy way to bring up your kids. If you drink alcohol, do so responsibly. Never, ever drink and go near the wheel of a car. Never, ever. Be sure your kids know this is your policy and how serious you are about drinking and driving. Consider abstaining from alcohol yourself—you may be surprised at how nice life is when you are consistently sober.

Make it a point to let your children hear you when you politely turn down drinks, especially when you're driving. This will clearly show them how easy it is to say "no" and still have a good time without alcohol.

Make substance abstinence for your kids, and perhaps for yourself, part of your family code of values. This is one of the big-gies, folks, right up there with building honesty, responsibility, and self-discipline. Set up a rule banning *all* kid substance use (including cigarettes) and stick to it. If you need to employ alcohol or drug screens to get their attention and motivation, do it. Don't back down on this one!

The Law of
Winning the War:

Pick Your
Battles Wisely

Have a couple of really good kids but feel like you've no energy left to enjoy them? You may be trying to win every fight instead of picking your battles. Learn to choose what's really important to focus on and what to let go. Trust your kids as well as your instincts. Learn how to negotiate and be realistic to avoid power plays. Hey, you may even have some fun!

Colleen, mother of 11-year-old Maggie and 7-year-old Trent, was determined to raise her kids right. As a widow and single mom, Colleen felt significant responsibility to be both mother and father to the children, to be there for homework and sports, and to serve as confidante. She also had great expectations for Maggie and Trent. Their grades were usually solid A's and B's, their rooms were kept clean, and, like it or not, they were expected to help around the house. When their dad was alive, she had the backup of a partner and could discuss disciplinary tools to use, as well as what was important and what wasn't in terms of raising the kids. But in the 2 years since Jack's death, Colleen had to find an equilibrium that worked for her and the children. Times were tough following the passing of their father, but they had made it through both financially and emotionally. Colleen kept her kids on a schedule that helped to keep them on track. Schoolwork was finished right after dinner, and a bedtime curfew was adhered to.

However, as time passed since the death of their father and the children matured, Colleen saw the kids becoming resentful of some of her rules and regulations. Maggie began to give her a hard time about making her bed in the morning and cleaning up her room each night, and she fussed when told to get off the telephone. Trent began to stall about beginning his homework right after dinner since his favorite TV show began at that time. Now, don't get me wrong, Colleen's children were good kids but had become a bit rambunctious as they grew. Maggie definitely was displaying a mind of her own, beginning to make decisions on dress, friends, and interests, as well as whether or not she was going to follow her mother's rules and requests. The compliance of her early years was fading, and Maggie's budding independence was blossoming. Trent was like a shadow, and as he watched his big sister's behavior, he tried to follow her path. It would have been comical for an outsider to see the two of them in action. It was like Pete and Repeat—whenever Maggie stood up to her mom or disagreed on an issue, Trent had to find his own problem to discuss or way to refuse. Luckily Colleen was wise enough to see what he was doing, but it was still wearing to be fighting battles all on her own.

Colleen brought the two kids in to see me, and we discussed what was happening in the family. Maggie did have some legitimate gripes—Mom was picky, and the kid made her point by bringing up specific examples of Colleen's inflexibility. Trent basically went along with the show—he mimicked his sister but was able to describe some situations when he felt that Mom was unfair. Colleen didn't disagree with the kids—after Jack's passing it was necessary for her to keep the boat afloat, and it was in her nature to resort to schedules and discipline. That worked great while the kids were younger, but they were now challenging her inflexibility, and rightly so. Things had changed over the past 2 years, but Colleen hadn't.

I explained to her that her initial reaction to being the only parent was a good one. Many people fall into depression following the loss of a spouse and become too flexible with rules and expectations. At least Colleen had kept the kids on track at home and at school. However, it was now time to back off a bit—the children had proven that they could make wise, responsible choices and had shown a good work ethic as well as study skills. In the big scheme of things, did it really matter if their beds were made before school or that they ate only one snack before dinner rather than two?

My point was that Colleen was on the path to winning the battle but losing the war. Now, I'm not saying that child rearing is combat—but it certainly can be a constant challenge! And there are battles to be won or lost, many on a single day. But the wise parent is one who picks the skirmishes carefully. Will this particular behavior make a difference in a week, month, or year? If not, perhaps it's best to let it go and give the kid the choice as to making the bed or not, wearing shorts or long pants to school, or talking to members of the opposite sex on the telephone. Consider whether the issue is worthy of a confrontation—

if you argue about everything, then the kids will begin to tune you out. This is analogous to parents who frequently yell at their children. Soon, the kids don't listen, as they don't know when to take it seriously. If *everything* is a battle, perhaps you're picking too many issues to get involved in.

What really matters? Take a good look at your children. Decide on the areas in which you can trust their judgment, and perhaps back off a notch or two. On those issues where they still show impulsivity or poor judgment, then it's best to stay involved and to continue to call the shots. If you don't back off when it's appropriate, not only will your kids become resentful, but it's incredibly wearing on the parent to be on red-alert status about the small, medium, and big stuff. Keep to the latter—focus on what really matters. The acid test, in my opinion, is if the kid's choice won't really matter in a month or two, then consider letting him call the shot this time around. If it is a significant area of behavior (such as completing homework or not), then of course you must put your foot down and stick with it. But consider letting go of some of the responsibility and choose your battles more carefully— you just may be surprised at how well the kids do, as well as how they listen when you do lay down the law on the big stuff!

LIVING THE LAW

Negotiate. Decide on which behaviors are negotiable and which are not. Negotiable issues can be curfews, television-watching time, or when to do homework (before or after dinner). Nonnegotiable rules need to be the important ones that involve health, safety, homework completion, politeness—basically the laws found in this book. Other than these areas, try to be flexible and grow the rules with the child.

Be realistic. What may have been appropriate to focus on at a younger age may become negotiable and perhaps not nearly as important a few years later. Consider your individual child, his personality, friends, and environment. Perhaps you, as a kid, may not have been interested in wearing the latest styles, but if your daughter is surrounded by fashion model wannabes, then you may have to give her a break in this area. As long as her dress does not exceed the mores in your family's code of values, it's probably best to let her exert some independence in this area.

Figure out what really matters. Put some thought into what's really important to you as a parent and stick with the program. Some folks value spending time with the kids in play, attending a place of worship as a family unit, volunteering, getting household chores done, or pursuing lessons to teach the kids specific skills or knowledge. Whatever is important to the healthy development of the family should be focused upon, and you should call the shots on those issues.

Stop reminding. Picking your battles also entails how you proceed once you've decided to dig in your heels and demand compliance from your children. Don't repeat yourself when you've asked your child to do something. Make the request, remind him of the consequence if it is not heeded, and move on. In this way battles stay battles and do not evolve into wars. So many kids have described to me how much the constant reminding and nagging aggravates them—it's almost more annoying than the issue at hand!

Avoid power plays. Although you are accustomed to being in control, please do so gracefully. Telling a kid to "do it because I said so" is not nearly as effective as describing why it should be done. Being curt or nasty usually leads to even greater kid defiance, not the compliance that you are striving to achieve. It's all in the presentation, and if you can present your argument concisely and politely, you'll have a much greater chance of being heard and perhaps avoiding a skirmish.

Develop your skill in picking battles. As with acquiring any new behavior, it takes practice, compromise, and setting it as a goal to be attained. Try to keep a flexible approach as the kids grow older and the situation merits change. And you may find that you're able, as your children move into middle and high school, to let them call more of the shots, especially if they've shown good judgment in the past. Even kids who were impulsive and undependable in preschool and grade school can develop responsible behavior and attitudes, especially if you've employed a behavioral system as discussed in the laws of this book. Be responsive to the changes in your children's development of self-discipline. If the kid is making sense in his argument, it may be time for you to reassess the situation and to declassify it as grounds for doing battle.

LAW #10

The Law of Involvement:

Become a Hands-On Parent

Wouldn't it be great if you could vaccinate your child against peer pressure . . . drugs . . . academic underachievement? You can. I've found that your best shot is to be involved with your kids at home, in the neighborhood, and at school. Know who your kids hang out with and where they go, stay in touch with their friends' parents, and have the guts to set up and maintain curfews.

nvolved parenting is the only way to go. You can't get around it—parents who watch their kids closely and are involved in their neighborhood and school activities tend to raise children who walk the straight and narrow. Kids whose parents look the other way or depend upon someone else to "raise" their children pay big time—especially when the child reaches the tween or teen years.

I've seen this for years in my clinical practice and preach the value of involved, hands-on parenting whenever I get the chance. I discuss this with parents in my office as well as at seminars. What does being an "involved parent" entail? This is a hands-on approach to raising kids. It necessitates considerable parental attention and participation, letting kids know that you are watching their behavior, raising the bar in terms of expectations as appropriate, and making clear and fair rules for the children.

Parents often have lots of questions about involved parenting, and below are the most common ones that I'm asked about this parenting style.

Is involved parenting the same as strict parenting? Is it the same as authoritative or autocratic parenting?

Involved parenting is akin to strict parenting in many ways—rules are adhered to, behaviors are watched closely, and the parent often participates in the child's activities. But hands-on parents are not strict or rigid—they are flexible, fair, and consistent.

Where authoritative or autocratic parents do not take into account the feelings, wishes, and nature of the individual child, involved parents do. Knowing that each child needs freedoms and opportunities to explore, yet reasonable guidelines, hands-on parents succeed because they take their children's ideas into account when setting rules and consequences. They may be viewed as strict by their children because of their consistency of discipline, but hands-on parents are not seen as robotic and punishing like autocratic parents or as controlling and intrusive as authoritative parents. Involved parents are flexible—but the zone of acceptable behavior is clear to the child. Parents can be authoritative or autocratic and *not* be involved (setting rules but not following through). Involved parents create rules that are fair, *and* they take the time to follow through by paying attention to kid behaviors such as curfews, TV viewing, and school grades.

Does the involvement refer just to discipline?

No, it doesn't. Hands-on parenting means follow-through, consistency, and participation. At times it will involve discipline, but it often concerns other aspects of child rearing. For example, conferencing with teachers is indicative of a hands-on parent, as is setting the rule that homework should be done well. Hands-on parenting doesn't stop with setting rules—it continues with monitoring, enforcement, and followup. The hands-on parent remembers to check the child's planner every day to see if the work has been completed and is ready to be turned in. The hands-on parent takes action, in conjunction with the teacher, to institute a new homework plan if the child isn't living up to his end of the bargain. The hands-on parent doesn't do the work for the child but does establish the structure for the work to take place.

Does involvement mean lots of extracurricular activities?

Not necessarily—only if you and the child desire to sign up for them. Sure, it's great for your kid to learn a new skill or to develop a talent. But hands-on parenting does not necessitate carting your kid around from activity to activity. It refers to your awareness of what your child is doing and that you are supervising his activities, whether these are lessons, schoolwork, or neighborhood fun. In fact, kids seem to be overscheduled rather than not having enough to do. Give yourself a break and spend less time in the car and more at home!

Can parental involvement be overdone?

Sure, if the parent's behavior is stifling the child's independence, development of self-discipline, or social growth. Or if the bar is set too high for the individual child (grade expectations that are not reasonable) or the parental requirement is unreasonable (going along on dates with your 17-year-old daughter), then the involvement is more neurosis than good parenting. Folks need to pick their battles—I personally focus upon safety, academic achievement, social skill development, and responsibility issues, and stay flexible on others.

Do kids resent the involvement of hands-on parents?

No, especially if they are raised in this fashion and don't know better! I believe that children who are raised with clear, fair, and consistent rules that are adhered to by their hands-on parents thrive, although they may not want to admit that Mom's presence at Back to School night is important. Children who know that their folks are watching and are concerned understand just how far to push the limits and realize where their folks draw the line. Parents who are consistently inconsistent in their involvement (concerned today about homework but not necessarily tomorrow) are seen by kids as confusing and often as unfair.

Do children of involved parents rebel more than those raised by less observant folks?

Generally not—especially if Mom or Dad is fair in their hands-on tactics. Getting overinvolved or making mountains out of molehills may lead to resentment on the child's part, but if the parent is reasonable, this usually doesn't occur. It's interesting—I've had the opportunity to work with two generations of the same family in many cases (seeing the child as a teenager and then 10 years later with their own little ones), and many are choosing to raise their kids in a hands-on manner also.

Should parents continue the hands-on mode when the kids become teenagers?

Definitely—teens need as much parental involvement as possible. In fact, a study conducted by the Columbia University-based *National Center on Addiction and Substance Abuse* looked specifically at the effect of "hands-on" versus "hands-off" parenting on tween and teen behavior. Not surprisingly, the study found that kids who live in highly structured households (hands-on parenting) were at significantly lower risk for substance abuse and other risk-taking behaviors than were children who lived in less structured homes (hands-off parenting). The behaviors examined included smoking cigarettes, substance use and abuse, and other risk-taking behaviors by the children as well as by their friends.

What do hands-on parents do?

Take 30 seconds now to answer the questions in "Are You a Hands-On Parent?" to see what your parenting style is.

How did you fare? I have to admit that although I consider myself to be a very involved and observant parent (accused by my own kids of being a direct descendant of Attila the Hun), I blew it on the eating dinner together item. We *definitely* do not eat dinner together six nights a week. In fact, sometimes we don't have dinner at all, just everyone grabbing something from the refrigerator and running out of the house to be on time to an activity.

But I passed in all of the other categories. Fortunately, I can arrange my schedule to be home by three o'clock in the afternoon. I may be working in my den or at the computer or returning a client's phone call, but I'm there when the high school football team makes an impromptu visit to our backyard pool or a kid needs help with homework. My children have cell phones to use to call home when leaving a location, and the home answering machine allows them no excuse for not checking in and leaving a message if we are out. Consistent communication with teachers via report cards and progress reports have been excellent ways of staying up with my kids' school responsibilities, and teacher conferences have been necessary in the past.

But not every parent can be at home after school—many moms and dads work until late in the afternoon, and kids are often unsupervised between three and five o'clock. Aftercare and daycare programs are used by parents of young children but are often not available for

Are You a Hands-On Parent?

The following are the 12 indicators used in a study conducted by the Columbia University-based *National Center on Addiction and Substance Abuse*, which looked at the effect of two different parenting styles on tween and teen behavior. Answer the questions honestly and check the bottom of the list to see how you rate.

- Do you expect to be told where your child is going in the evening or on weekends and told the truth about this?
- Have you made it clear that you would be "extremely upset" to find your child using marijuana?
- Do you know where your child is at all times, particularly after school and on weekends?
- Do you monitor what your child is watching on television?
- Do you impose restrictions on the kind of music your child is allowed to buy?
- Are you very aware of how your child is doing in school?
- Do you monitor your child's Internet usage?
- Does your family typically have dinner together six nights a week?
- Does your child have a weekend curfew?
- Is an adult always at home when the child returns from school?
- Is your child responsible for completing regular chores?
- Do you make sure the television is not on during dinner?

According to the researchers, if you answered "yes" to at least 10 of the 12 questions, you're a hands-on parent. Keep up the good work! If you answered "yes" to 5 or fewer, you're a hands-off parent. The 25 Laws of Parenting are just what you and your kids need to get you more involved and keep your kids on track.

middle- and high-school youngsters. And most of these kids put up such a fuss about having to be supervised that parents usually cave in, letting them stay home alone, hoping for the best. If that's your situation, consider setting up a neighborhood network where your kids can stay at a friend's house after school, perhaps in exchange for your carpooling services in the morning. Or offer to babysit your neighbor's little ones on the weekend in exchange for supervising your tween or teen after school.

I believe that most parents can become more hands-on with a little effort and attention to the 12 questions listed in the quiz. Kids need weekend and weekday curfews, and these can be imposed, but be sure to be fair and consistent. Moving the computer to a more public spot in your home is a natural solution to monitoring Internet usage, and watching television with your kids discourages viewing inappropriate shows. Of course, making these changes may temporarily place you lower down on your child's popularity list, but that's okay. Your job as a parent is not to please your kids or to keep them happy or to provide them with a feeling of entitlement or privilege. Your priorities are to keep them safe and on track and teach them self-responsibility and frustration tolerance.

Hands-on parenting works. I see that every day in my clinical practice, and the research backs that up. Sure, it may take greater effort, attention, and involvement with your children on a daily basis, and your kids may not show gratitude or appreciation for your hard work. In fact, they may be downright indignant about your increased involvement! But dig your heels in and do what's right—your child's behavior, success, safety, and accomplishments will reflect your concern.

LIVING THE LAW

To become a more hands-on parent, check out these guidelines.

Don't set up too many activities for you or for your children. If you're overwhelmed, odds are that you may not be able to follow through and keep a good eye on what the kids are up to.

Don't just make new rules—be sure to follow through with them. Move the television or the computer to a public family area so that it's easier for you to be consistent in observing what your child is watching on TV or surfing on the Web.

Check on your kids' plans. When your grade schooler or middle schooler is visiting at a friend's house, call ahead and speak with a parent to make sure that the visit is acceptable and that the activities to be engaged in are reasonable. Be sure that the children will be supervised. Don't cave in when your kid accuses you of being overprotective. Don't buy into your child's statement that "Johnny's mother lets him walk across a six-lane highway to go to the mall." Most likely Johnny's mom doesn't allow it, or if she does, your kid shouldn't be hanging around with Johnny or his mom. With teenagers, check that they will actually be supervised by a parent at a sleepover or a party. Many will try to scam their folks into thinking that they are staying at each other's house for the night, when they are really planning to spend the night elsewhere in an unsupervised setting.

Be prepared to forfeit some of your freedoms in order to follow through with the family rules. For instance, if you're trying to work on the 12 indicators noted above, you shouldn't watch TV during dinner if the kids can't. If you say that you'll be home to supervise them after school or to pick them up at school, be there and be on time. When children can count on their folks to be involved, they can relax and more fully enjoy their childhoods.

LAW #11

The Law of Trusting Your Parenting Instincts:

Don't Cave In to Other Families' Rules

Sure, you wouldn't jump off a bridge just because your neighbor did, but would you live by their rules just because your kids want you to or because you're too embarrassed to disagree? That's what you may be doing if you're caving in to other families' rules and standards. Learn how to gracefully take the rap for being a bit overprotective and old-fashioned. The old adage is still true—better safe than sorry.

Okay, your 11-year-old daughter has just returned from school with a sleepover invitation from a new classmate. This is usually no problem, because you know and like your daughter's friends. But what do you do when the child is new to you, or even worse, when you go to pick up your child at her friend's house, and you discover that her parents have some very questionable attitudes in running their home.

Hopefully you've developed your family code of values well enough so that your child understands and abides by it in terms of behavior and safety issues. But what about your daughter's new friend—do she and her family respect the same values and rules?

Often, they won't—every family is different, and what's important to you may not carry the same weight with other parents. You may be a neat freak or stuck on nutritional issues but flexible when it comes to your kids' appearance or bedtimes. In my experience, things like that are usually not worth winning the battle and losing the war over. In other words, the small stuff can be seen as negotiable and shouldn't determine who your kids are allowed to hang out with when spending free time. Where the line should be drawn, though, is on the big stuff—issues of safety and morality.

Many of my clients face this type of conflict and come to see me in order to resolve problems before they get out of hand.

Kristin and her folks, Brenda and Mike, came to counseling to resolve budding conflicts regarding differences in how she was being raised in comparison with her two best friends, Jamie and Jeannie. The three girls, currently in the fourth grade at the same school, were practically joined at the hip. Together since kindergarten, they shared the joys and agonies of childhood and grew to depend upon one another for fun as well as support. Even the parents were close, carpooling to school and babysitting in a pinch, helping each other out when necessary. Two years ago, Jamie's parents separated and later divorced, but her mother stayed in close contact with the other families and promoted the relationship among the three girls.

In early grade school, when the kids tended to take their cues more from their folks than from their friends, the going was fairly smooth. As the girls went to parochial school and uniforms were mandatory, dress was not an issue, and extracurricular activities tended to revolve around dance and gymnastics. But as the children matured, Kristin's parents became uneasy with some of the changes that they were seeing in the trio. Jeannie began to wear makeup on the weekends, and Jamie's mother had apparently backed off of some of the rules regarding bedtime, telephone curfews, and TV/movie ratings. During sleepovers at her friends' homes, it wasn't unusual for Kristin to watch scary movies or the *Austin Powers* series, which Brenda and Mike found inappropriate. When the kid came home on Saturday morning with a truly expanded vocabulary (not to her parents' liking at all), Brenda had had enough. She felt that the other girls were moving too fast for her comfort zone and that Kristin needed some new guidelines. And that's when the family hit a speed bump.

Brenda and Mike found it tantamount to changing the rules of the game midway, since the three girls had always been able to do the same activities throughout their relationship. Kristin was angry when her folks began to restrict her visits with her two best friends, and she honestly felt that her parents were being unfair. That, of course, led to some talking back and eventually some heavy-duty timeouts. The family was getting nowhere with this issue, and they finally landed in my office.

After hearing all of their views—Mom's, Dad's, and Kristin's—it was apparent that compromise and communication were in order. First, Kristin needed to accept that her family had rules that were, apparently, different in some aspects from her friends'. Many values were shared, but some were different. Second, Brenda and Mike needed to prioritize what differences were really important and to focus upon those that involved Kristin's physical, moral, and emotional health.

Third, the parents needed to specify and clarify what were appropriate and inappropriate activities and behaviors for their daughter, without putting down or judging the other families' decisions. Last, Kristin, as the kid, would have to accept (notice that I didn't say *enjoy*) her parents' views and to tone down the grumping, griping, and complaining that "it's not fair." Fair or not, her folks were responsible for her upbringing, and if they didn't want their child to view horror flicks or R-rated movies, talk on the phone beyond curfew, or dress like a teenager at 10 years of age, that was their decision.

Brenda and Mike were also faced with the problem of describing their concerns and decisions to the other parents. We discussed the most politically correct ways of communicating their wishes, without appearing to be disparaging or judgmental. Kristin also would need to educate her friends about her new limits and help them to creatively find activities that were fun and acceptable to all three families. It was a learning process, and not totally comfortable, but they found that directly dealing with the issues, rather than dancing around them, was the most effective and efficient solution to this sticky problem.

As a parent, one of your most important roles is that of protector as well as provider. Being politely assertive, asking appropriate and pointed questions, and keeping a sense of humor as well as a sense of balance are requisite when guiding your children into and through friendships. Involvement with your children's friends is key in helping you to gain information upon which to base your judgments, and ultimately decisions, about acceptance of other families' rules.

LIVING THE LAW

Let's take a look at some of the forbidden fruit that may crop up at friends' homes and the best ways in which to handle these issues. Obviously, these will change as your child grows, but there are a few generic principles that I've found are applicable to most situations.

Take the rap for being nosy, overprotective, or neurotic. I've learned from my clinical practice that folks are much more open to dealing with your self-criticism than the perception of being criticized themselves. My personal favorite when I'm in this sticky situation is to begin the conversation with something like, "I know that this is a bit neurotic, but . . . " Or a good fallback is, "I admit, I'm known for my overprotectiveness, but . . . ," and then I fill in the blank with my concern. I might add, "Will the kids be allowed to watch R-rated or scary movies during the sleepover?" If the answer if "yes," then I'd request that something else be chosen, letting it be known that my kid scares easily and will be a frequent visitor to our bed for the next few weeks, which I would like to avoid. This tactic not only gives the other parent permission to consider me the loopy one, but it also provides the information that I need as well as sending the message that my child shouldn't be allowed an HBO free-for-all.

Be sure that your child is clear about the boundaries of acceptability. Give your child some credit, as well as responsibility, when it comes to staying within your guidelines. Your kid knows if she's allowed to wear makeup or go to the mall without an adult present. Expect her to follow your rules, or at least to call and ask permission for an exception to be made. Applaud her honesty when she volunteers information about changes in the evening's lineup—it takes guts to call the folks to ask if it's okay to include boys in the movie plans. That doesn't mean that you have to agree with the idea, but at least let her know that you appreciate her honesty and communication.

Never, ever be reticent to inquire about real or toy weapons. It's not only your right but also your responsibility to know if the kids will have access to BB guns, "toy" bows and arrows, or other play weapons. Many families do not allow their children to play with toy weapons, as the parents believe that these toys are "gateways" to the real McCoy, or that playing with a toy bow and arrow can be dangerous. (My own son, at age 3, was struck in the eye by a friend's toy arrow—

luckily it was a small cut and did not damage his vision.) If a weapon-free environment (be it toy or real) is part of your family's code of values, then this issue is most likely worth digging in your heels.

Many of the moms and dads that I work with are concerned not only with play weapons but also with real guns being in the host homes. I've found that it's usually best to be direct and forward about this issue—no beating around the bush here. Ask the host if they possess a gun and how it is stored. If you feel even the least bit uncomfortable with the answer, don't allow your child to visit their home. It's just not worth your worry and the possibility of injury. Perhaps the weapon can be removed during your child's visit, but many folks won't go to the trouble to do so, or you may have doubts that they will actually follow through with the temporary removal.

Let them explore, but get to know their friends. Socialization at every age is important to your child's cognitive and emotional development. You can only be the den mother so many times, and then you have to let go and allow your child to explore other people's homes, values, and rules. To lessen your anxiety, try to get to know your child's friends and their parents intimately—via telephone, personal visits, play dates together at the park, or volunteering at school activities and field trips. With little ones you'll keep a close eye on their friends' environments, and most likely you'll migrate to interfamily relationships that reflect your own family's code of values.

Give in a little. As your kids grow, you should never allow them to stay in a situation that you feel is immoral or unsafe, but you may have to give a little when it comes to the smaller stuff. For instance, perhaps the kids will be offered more junk food than you're comfortable with, or the bedtime is too late for your taste. Think about it—will this really hurt your child a week from now? Probably not, as long as you let her know that this is not what you would allow in your home. Tell her that other people have different values and rules, and within certain parameters you're willing to let her experience them. If you see, though, that your kid is becoming rebellious to your own rules or developing an "attitude" because the Jones family does it differently, then it may be time to tone down her visits with the Jones clan.

Finally, stick to the five W's—the who, what, where, when, and why of the visit. Especially as your children grow into the tween and teen years, when kids start to clam up, it may be all you may get from the kid. But every time that kid leaves the house you absolutely need to know:

- Who's he with?

- What's he doing?

- Where will he be the whole time? (Make sure you know if he's getting in the car with older kids or heading somewhere to hang out other than where you drop him off.)

- When will this happen and when will they be done?

- Why in the heck do they want to do it anyway?

Don't hesitate to verify these plans with the other kids' parents.

Let your kid know that ultimately he is responsible for his behavior and that later and greater freedoms (attending sleepaway camp, driving the car) will depend upon the honesty and common sense shown now while visiting with friends. I can't tell you the number of times that I have tried to make this point to an 11-, 12-, or 13-year-old. All of them eventually understand what I am talking about, but some of the especially ornery ones fight acceptance of my point. The principle at stake is that parental trust doesn't just happen overnight. It is based upon Mom and Dad watching the kid's behaviors, choices, and motivations throughout his lifetime.

Children who tend to fudge, omit, or downright lie about details of their behavior or whereabouts are not likely to be trusted as teenagers. I tell them that Mom and Dad are not dumb—they know that the best predictor of the future is the past. And that although people do change (thank goodness!), the process tends to take a while; often parents need enough time to view a pattern of change in behavior to believe that the child has shown consistent good judgment and now truly believes that honesty is the best policy.

On the other hand, kids who can be counted upon to do what they promise to do, to be where they say they will be, and to communicate effectively with their parents are often granted many freedoms and choices about who their friends are and what they are allowed to do. So, if you find yourself in a discussion with your 11-year-old about whether she'll be allowed to get her driver's license at age 16, emphasize that there is a strong correlation between her current behavior and what her future privileges will be.

LAW #12

The Law of Trust but Verify:

Don't Be Afraid to Snoop

Of all the parenting issues that I deal with, this is one of the stickiest. Of course you want to trust your child and treat his possessions as private, but what if the kid's behavior raises significant suspicion? Does that give you the right to rifle through the bedroom reading notes or journals, or search drawers for drugs or paraphernalia? You're darn tootin' it does! Sometimes we have to save our kids even from themselves, and if you must ruffle their feathers in the process, so be it.

This is the law that always sparks the most debate. It's also the one that parents are most relieved to read, because it gives them permission to be parents again!

One of the most important parenting responsibilities is the safety of your child. And this law makes it clear that it is your right and responsibility to check on your child's safety by knowing what your child is getting into—involvement with friends, attendance and performance at school, and following your family's rules. But this doesn't give you carte blanche to invade your child's privacy when it's not warranted. Sometimes you'll know straight up what your kid is into, but at other times he may be somewhat secretive. All parents have been faced with anxiety about their children's secret lives, and when given the chance to invade, some do and some don't.

Let's say that you come home from work, lay your coat down on the table, and notice a half-opened crumpled piece of notebook paper, clearly written in your 12-year-old daughter's handwriting and begging to be read by you. It's just sitting there. If she really wanted to keep it private, wouldn't she have either thrown it away or put it in her bedroom? Is this her preteen way of asking you to read it, is it a cry for help, or a method of communicating with you? Or is she just so darn self-absorbed at this time in her life that she either didn't notice that she left it out or couldn't bother to dispose of it?

You have a decision to make and not much time to make it. Softball practice is over in a half-hour and soon she'll be bursting through the front door demanding dinner. What do you do? Compromise your trust relationship by snooping and reading the note, or leave it alone, forever wondering if it would have given you a window into your daughter's private world, one that she's been keeping more to herself as she grows toward adolescence.

To Snoop or Not to Snoop?

Let's say that she's a good kid with decent grades but could stand to study more. Lately it seems that she's living on the phone and recently has been taking the cordless to her room to chat with her friends. And then there's *that boy* from outside the neighborhood who tends to call just a little too late each night—what's *his* mother thinking?! Oh, you could go on and on, whipping yourself into a frenzy before you know it. Why did she leave that darn note out in the first place? Should you snoop and read it, or resist the temptation and respect her privacy? Tough spot to be in but take solace in realizing that you are not alone.

Virtually every parent will have to make this type of decision, and trust me, it won't be a one-timer. As your children grow and develop, make friends on their own (at times without your input or control), and communicate less with you and more with their buds, you'll often feel left out of the loop or that your advice is not wanted or heeded. That's normal—kids like to be independent, in control of their friendships, and confident in their decisions and choices. What's also normal, though, is for children to make some poor judgment calls, to use less common sense at 12 than they did at 8 years of age, and to cave in to peer pressure. And the worst part of this developmental process is that often the most important decisions (whether to experiment with drugs, to ride in cars with older friends, to skip the study session and just copy someone else's paper) are the ones that you are not involved with or informed of. Just when children need to be communicating with you more, they generally clam up, leaving the concerned parent guessing about their child's world and decision making.

Kids can be incredibly disorganized, lazy, and sloppy. Even those who are trying to keep things away from their parents often leave out very incriminating evidence. Trust me, they are generally *not* leaving it out on purpose—the phone probably rang and the note from the friend discussing the beer bash on Friday night was inadvertently left on the kitchen table. Take 16-year-old Nelson, who left some marijuana and rolling papers under the passenger seat of his mother's car. When Mom found them, she considered alerting the police but chose to flush the stuff down the toilet instead. And Nelson had the gall to be angry with her for "throwing away his perfectly good pot!" So don't assume that evidence you find was purposely left out for you and is a "call for help." It may be, but most often it's an oversight and the kid will be either embarrassed or furious that you found it.

Very smart, manipulative kids may even go so far as to try to pawn off their bad behavior onto you. Stephanie, at the tender age of 13, was a pro at diverting the focus from herself. Steph's parents had been concerned that she was sneaking out the window at night and had warned her that they would be watching her behavior closely. Although a pro at diversionary tactics, Stephanie was a slob at heart and tended to leave her stuff all over the house. So when Dad saw a suspicious-looking note on the foyer floor, he opened and read it. As it turned out, it concerned that night's agenda for a quick run through the neighborhood with the hopes of meeting up with some of her friends. When her father handed her the note and demanded an explanation, the ever-on-the-offensive Steph deftly came back with, "How could you read my note? That was my property!" Boy, did she appear offended as she tried to seal the deal with, "I'm really angry with you—you owe me an apology." Right. Here's a kid who was plotting to sneak out, was given fair warning from her folks that they would be watching her behavior very closely, and she gets her nose bent out of shape just because Dad read a note that she left on the floor. Nice try, kid.

Kids can be very sneaky. So if the situation arises where you believe that your child is considering or engaging in dangerous or illegal activity, you must take action. First, try to open discussion about the

Explaining the Law to Your Kids

Tell your children that if they want you to respect their privacy, to trust them, and to leave their stuff alone, they should do the following:

Keep their rooms clean. Don't give us an excuse to rifle through it.

Keep up the grades. We believe that if you're trying hard in school, you're probably not getting into too much trouble elsewhere. Displaying good judgment at school suggests using common sense with friends and mature decision making in general.

Talk our ears off. Don't just say "fine" when we ask how school was that day, or "nothing" when we question what occurred in class. Talk about anything—the weather, what you want for your birthday, what's cooking with the neighbors, a school project, or upcoming weekend plans. Who knows, you may find that you actually enjoy speaking with us!

The more you communicate with us, the less we'll feel that you are being secretive and perhaps hiding something. The more comfortable we are with you, the less we'll feel the need to snoop. Show us the yearbook before your friends begin to sign it. That way we can take our time to look at the pictures and to get an overview of the school year. Or, if it's already been passed by your friends and you feel uncomfortable with our reading it, you can supervise our perusal of the book, limiting us to the pictures or comments from certain friends or teachers. We will respect your privacy as long as you're working with us.

Don't leave their personal things around the house. Your journal contains your private thoughts, but it is also your responsibility to keep it private and in the bedroom.

Choose their friends wisely. You are judged by the company you keep, and even though we may trust you, we may not appreciate your buddy's lack of curfew or class clown reputation.

Respect the privacy of the other family members. You can't expect to get what you aren't willing to give. If you want privacy for your possessions, show us the same amount of respect for ours.

inappropriate behavior, including what your concerns are and what you want to see changed. If that doesn't work and you're still worried that your child may engage in illegal, immoral, or dangerous activity, then you may need to snoop. This can take the form of reading the diary, checking the kid's pockets for notes or drugs, looking over e-mails sent or received (or at least limiting or disabling the Internet), and monitoring telephone conversations. Don't expect your child to be happy about any of this—he will most likely be angry and upset with your snooping, but remember who drew "first blood" and started the whole mess—the child!

LIVING THE LAW

So, let's get down to some basic "to snoop or not to snoop" guidelines.

Respect your child's privacy and possessions. Until your son or daughter proves to you that they are exhibiting poor judgment in significant and important areas of their life, you should respect their privacy. Trust takes a long time to develop in family (and other) relationships, yet it can be so quickly destroyed. Remember that, and also remember your own childhood. Did your Mom or Dad have a habit of rifling through your stuff, either covertly or overtly? How did you feel about it? Probably not good, and you resented the invasions of your privacy, especially if they weren't warranted!

Clarify what is and what is not snooping behavior on your part. Some behaviors that are considered as nosy by kids may be thought of as appropriate by their folks. (See "What Kids Consider to Be Snooping" on page 104.) Be sure to check this out with your own children so that everyone is square on the rules. Discuss what is private and what isn't—the child's diary, journal, yearbook, notes from friends, and e-mails sent and received. How about possessions stored in dresser drawers, under the bed, or in clothing pockets?

Even if you do discuss this, some sticky situations may still crop up. What happens if the kid asks you to do his laundry and in emptying his jeans pockets you find a $50 bill? Problem is, he shouldn't have a penny to his name. Or you are listening to the messages on the family answering machine and one of your daughter's friends comments on the outfit that she wore to the party last night, the one that

What Kids Consider to Be Snooping

From your kid's point of view, their stuff is off limits unless they give you specific permission to look at, read, or listen to it. And should you slip up and break that trust, they are quite unforgiving. All of the years of affording them privacy can be tarnished by being caught red-handed reading a single note or eavesdropping on a phone call. Trust me, they will *never* forget it and will bring it up at every opportunity. Here's the scoop on what most kids consider to be inappropriate snooping.

- Reading the yearbook without their express permission (especially after it has been signed by friends, often with off-color remarks).
- Listening in on telephone conversations (either standing by the phone or actually picking up the receiver without their knowledge).
- Taping telephone conversations.
- Reading e-mail or hovering over IM chatting on the Internet.
- Listening to private conversations when friends are over.
- Checking through drawers, closets, or under the bed or mattress.
- Looking through photo albums and boxes.
- Reading journals or diaries.

However, if your child gives you permission to look through the yearbook, for example, and you run into some embarrassing stuff—it's probably best to keep that to yourself. If you tease or make a big deal about it, odds are that you will not be invited to see next year's edition!

you expressly told her not to go to. Or while helping your 8-year-old clean out his room, you stumble upon a Game Boy cartridge that you know doesn't belong to him, and the family has a rule prohibiting borrowing toys or possessions from other kids. I believe that these situations are fair game for parents to deal with as part of the *Don't Be Afraid to Snoop* law. In these cases, the child either knows about or has asked for your involvement and therefore your "finds" are not the fruit of snooping. They are the result of carelessness on your kid's part.

Decide when you must take action. Although the goal is to trust and respect your child's choices, possessions, and activities, the line is crossed when the kid ventures into behaviors that are either dangerous physically or emotionally, or when illegal actions are being contemplated. These are important areas and cannot be overlooked. Your parental obligations are to provide, guide, and protect. If your child is placing herself in harm's way, you must intervene. And that may involve some serious snooping. What might trigger immediate action?

- Doing or dealing drugs
- Drinking alcohol or huffing inhalants
- Sneaking out and joyriding in Dad's car
- Running away from home as a solution to family squabbles or a reaction to being grounded for missing curfew
- Skipping school or classes
- "Chatting" on the Internet with strangers, especially if personal meetings are suggested

These are the types of *significant and important* issues that need to be addressed—when the kid has provided evidence that something dangerous or illegal is happening or about to occur. As a concerned parent, you must intervene. But before you dig through the dresser drawers, check for the journal under the mattress, or explore the depths of your son's book bag, it's important to confront the child directly, giving him the option of 'fessing up before you use surreptitious investigative tactics.

Use above-board communication to deal with the issue. If you get wind that Junior is using drugs, you must do something about it. Although some kids can "experiment" with substances, decide that it's a stupid idea, and move on, many get in over their heads. As a mom and a psychologist, I take a very dim view of child substance use and suggest that other parents do the same (as discussed in Law #8: The Law of Abstinence). Confront your child with your evidence and concerns but don't expect an immediate confession. If you find yourself getting nowhere in the discussion, drop the debate and take the kid to the pediatrician's office for a drug screen (kicking and screaming if need be). He will be less than thrilled with the idea and with you, but at least you're being honest and direct with him, even though he's been sneaky and deceptive with you.

Trust your gut instinct. If your middle schooler, for instance, starts acting sketchy about school and you get that *feeling* that something just isn't right (plus your best friend saw the kid hanging around the convenience store at lunchtime), ask him if he's been skipping and allow him the opportunity to salvage your trust. If he 'fesses up, there should be a consequence given, plus a failsafe school attendance system instituted to make sure that he doesn't play hooky again. If he is still in denial mode, check with the school attendance officer to get the facts (whether your child wants you to or not—remember he started this!). Then either apologize for your error if you are wrong, or institute the negative consequence if the kid has been skipping school.

Protect your child. Staying on top of your child's behavior may be tough, but try to keep the communication open, especially when you suspect that something is awry. If you continue to receive denials, counterattacks, or red-herring attempts to sidetrack you from the issue (be it sneaking out, drugs, skipping school, dating without permission), and direct discussion with your kid isn't working, you may need to be sneaky yourself. Hey, you've given the kid fair warning and he is continuing his involvement in dangerous, illegal, or highly inappropriate activities. Remember, sometimes we have to protect our children even from themselves.

LAW #13

The Law of Politeness:

Insist on Manners

Does it really matter if your child talks back, is a little snippy with you, or is generally obnoxious around adults? You bet it does. A child who never learns how to be polite will become a teenager who has trouble making friends and an adult who makes a poor impression. It may seem old-fashioned, but there's no better way to help your child make friends and influence people than to teach him good manners.

Picture this—the family is at Grandma and Grandpa's house for dinner. You're helping to set the table, your 14-year-old is yakking to a friend on the telephone, and your 8-year-old is watching television. Not knowing what's about to happen, Grandma tries to begin a conversation with your son, who's glued to the tube. At first he seems not to hear Grandma, but after she repeats herself, he tells her, "Hush, I'm watching TV." Now, some grandmas would clobber the kid while others would give him a big piece of their mind. But your mom looks stunned, as if the rude remark cut through her like a knife. Embarrassed, and feeling bad for your mother, you reprimand the kid, hoping for a sincere apology. But he adds insult to injury by noting that you tell him to hush, shush, be quiet, or even shut up when he's interrupting you at home. All of which may be true, but you didn't need Grandma to hear that. Her feelings are hurt, you're disappointed and angry with your son, and he's fuming because you're being hypocritical. Ever been there—in a sticky, humiliating situation where your child has been so rude to another that you want to slide under the rug? We all have.

Ready for some introspection? Think about the way *all* of your family members treat each other. Consider all the verbalizations, actions, ignoring, and responses that occur daily in your home. Now how would you feel if your employer, coworkers, neighbors, or friends could see a video of how your family members treat each other? Would it be something that you would be proud of or would it be humiliating and more than a tad embarrassing?

Why is it that we can be so rude, short-tempered, and impatient with the folks that we love the most, yet would *never* consider behaving in this manner with people that we are not related to? The answer lies in the dynamics of family life. We *have* to put up with one another, no matter what. Most family members admit to loving each other, if not exactly liking the other guy every single moment. In other words, we're kind of stuck with a grumpy Grandpa, a nagging Mom, an inconsiderate older sister, or a rambunctious little brother. They're not going anywhere and neither are we. This leads to a tendency to take one another for granted. That's normal and part of the nature of family life in most homes. We are not on our best behavior because we are so used to each other, assume that members will always be there, and are often so absorbed in our own needs and activities that we cannot see beyond the tips of our collective noses.

That often leads to a distinct family dynamic that is impolite, rude, or even offensive. In other words, we get relationship-lazy, and it's an insidious process. Not only are the kids culprits but so are Mom and Dad. Many parents barely get in a few sentences to each other, let alone polite conversation, before dinner has to be made, dishes done, homework supervised, and baths completed. Often children see their folks barking out commands to one another with rarely a civil word spoken. And these are not necessarily folks whose marriages are in trouble—they are just too busy, preoccupied, or stressed out to take the time to see how they are miscommunicating and too distant, lazy, or frightened to make some changes.

And then there are the kids. There's usually a lot of demanding and insisting going on, as well as grabbing and bossing. And that's just the preschoolers! Older kids can get downright nasty—cursing, name calling and teasing. And don't forget that ignoring is one of the most hurtful of behaviors—not being answered suggests that you're not deserving of a response. Or consider the "grunters"—questions may be answered with incomprehensible mutterings or sounds, basically making effective communication impossible.

Bad Manners Cost Your Kids Big-Time

I've found that children who are allowed to grow up engaging in rude, disrespectful, or impolite behavior are generally not well liked by others, as kids and later as adults. Self-esteem problems often result when peers avoid your child, and it's tough to change others' perceptions once your kid has been marked as rude or disrespectful. That's why it's important to confront the issue *now* when your child is sarcastic, caustic, or terminally impolite to family members or friends. Trust me, you're not doing him a favor by looking the other way, as these inappropriate habits are so easily formed yet so difficult to break.

If this sounds a bit like your children, please listen up. It's probably time to tone down rudeness in your home. Sometimes it may seem easier to ignore inappropriate behavior than to confront it. But in the long run you usually pay in spades for this laid-back, hope-it-goes-away-on-it's-own attitude. So let's take a look at what you should focus on in order to help change the way that your kids interact with others.

LIVING THE LAW

Teach the magic words. *Please, thank you,* and *excuse me* are still the basics of a polite vocabulary, but don't fall into the trap of believing that just because you remind your kids to use these words that they will do so automatically. As with any habit, it takes consistency to instill a new behavior. Expect your children to need consistent reminders until the magic words become second nature. Discuss with your kids what words you'd like them to use to get your attention—instead of interrupting, say "excuse me." It's important for parents to regularly use these respectful words and phrases themselves when interacting with their children—modeling goes a long way toward teaching, reinforcing, and maintaining polite verbiage and behavior.

Coach your kids to ask, not demand. Children get into the habit of *insisting* on privileges or your attention, rather than coming across as *requesting* it. Although their intentions may be appropriate (they think that they are asking, not demanding), many don't understand how their verbiage is perceived by others. Teach them that a request is something that usually is in question form (May I please . . .), rather than a statement (Give me the . . .). That's a safe way of assuring that they'll be perceived as asking, rather than as demanding. Most folks I know become ornery when kids tell them what's going to happen

("I'm going to the mall.") rather than asking for permission ("May I please borrow the car?"). It's really the same process but put differently, and it results in more parental cooperation since the child appears to be more respectful when asking than when demanding.

Focus on tone of voice. Many children have no clue how they are perceived by others. Little ones can appear to be whiney when they believe that they are just expressing their feelings, and teens often seem argumentative when they're trying to make a point. Teach your kids that they are responsible for both their intent as well as the way that they come across to others. Stop it by pointing out the tone and its inappropriateness. Say, "You're whining. If you'd like me to help you, you must ask politely," or "I know you're upset, but we don't use that tone of voice in our house." That's a life lesson that is invaluable—many adults ruin perfectly good relationships by relating in an inappropriate tone of voice, pitch, or volume. Better to learn this skill now as a youngster than to pay the price later as an adult!

Teach the "I message" technique. We all become angry or frustrated by others' behaviors once in a while, and for some kids, it's an almost daily occurrence. Instead of allowing them to lash out, teach your children the "I message" technique of describing what is bothering them. The basic structure of this technique is to state "I feel _____ when you _____." For example, calmly stating "I get mad when you come into my room and mess with my stuff without permission" is significantly more palatable (and effective) than hollering "Get out of my room, you moron!" If nothing else, the perpetrator will get the blame from Mom or Dad, and the victim looks like a cool cucumber. And fights occur much less frequently when the annoying party is either ignored or given an "I message" than when they are attacked. Often this is seen as provocation and retaliation follows. The "I message" should also include what the child would like the other to do. "Please knock before entering," or "Ask to play my Game

Boy, don't just take it" are statements that lead to better communication than verbal or physical attacks.

Insist on formal meets and greets. Even though this has become less and less common these days, I suggest to parents that they should assume that a formal introduction is preferable when it comes to meeting new people, especially adults. Mr. or Mrs., Coach or Doctor are all appropriate ways for children to speak to adults who are not family members. If the new friend wishes to be called something less formal, "Miss Sally" may be appropriate for little kids, or perhaps the person's first name if it is a very close acquaintance.

Dial up manners. Teach your children that if they are to answer the telephone, it must be done politely. "Davis residence" is not only polite but also lets the caller know whether the correct number has been dialed. Ask your child *not* to give out his first name, as the caller may be a stranger and shouldn't be given this information. And anyone who answers the telephone (yes, Mom or Dad included) should be expected to write down any messages taken and to give these to the intended person in a timely manner. If there's no time to write the message, then it should be allowed to go to voice mail or the answering machine. When phoning out, instruct your kids that they should first introduce themselves and then ask for their friend. "Hi, this is Matt. Is Mike home?" presents beautifully and gets the message across clearly. "Yo, big Mike there?" is less than impressive and just may turn Mike's folks off to the point of thinking twice before letting their kid play with your little heathen.

Use politically correct ways to decline an invitation. Learning to politely say "no" to an invitation is often a challenge, but there are savvy ways to deal with sticky situations. Your child doesn't want to hurt her friend's feelings. Teach her how to buy some "thinking time" by saying, "I'll have to check with my parents first." Then you can talk about the situation in a calm manner and together determine how it can best be handled without hurting feelings or appearing rude.

LAW #14

The Law of Compassion:

Teach Empathy and Volunteerism

If kids seem more selfish today, maybe it's because they spend so much time traveling in packs of other kids, pretty much doing things for enjoyment or their own personal entertainment. Empathy is one of the most teachable of emotions—but your child must be given the opportunity to learn it. No excuses, please—teach your kids compassion by volunteering with them, donating family time and perhaps a bit of your own resources. Discuss, teach, and live gratitude, and so will your children.

Some friends of ours have made such a strong impression on my family that they've convinced me to make an addition to my list of parenting priorities. Providing discipline, structure, involvement, and limit setting were always my primary focus, but these folks added a new dimension to what I now believe to be mandatory for raising good kids. And that element focuses upon compassion, empathy, and volunteerism. Let me tell you about this family.

Roger is an insurance broker and his wife, Gina, a fifth-grade teacher. They have eight children—Daniel, Scott, Christopher, Maggie, Rena, Max, and Barbara. Oh yeah, and Jimmy—the baby, who tends to get lost in the commotion of everyday life. Really nice kids, all with their quirks and challenging personality features, including a few who can be downright ornery at times. But there is one thing about Roger and Gina's brood that I admire above all—most have an exquisite compassion for others. In talking with the parents, I recognize their own empathy for people who have less, their willingness to take time out of busy schedules to volunteer in the community, and the moral conviction to teach these values to their children.

Notice that I said that *most* of the children behave compassionately—let me explain. Of the eight kids, six are right in there with their folks when it's time to help others or to give of themselves. Even 2-year-old Jimmy has been known to offer his teddy when a sibling is crying or hurt. But Maggie and Scott seem to be cut out of a slightly different cloth. Sure, they've observed their family helping others for years, just as their siblings have, but somehow it didn't stick quite as firmly as it has with the others. These two are obviously just going through the motions—serving food once a month at a local soup kitchen and gathering labels and newspapers to donate to their school. But they just don't appear to take joy in their giving; it's more an act of following their parents' behavior because the folks are watching. I've concluded that there's only so much one can do to nurture nature, and Maggie and Scott appear to be more self-absorbed than their siblings. But they are still benefiting from the training they are receiving by engaging in acts of volunteerism and giving to the community. Hopefully, as they mature, the empathy will internalize and become second nature.

How, you might ask, can two working parents of eight find the time to volunteer and give to others? Well, they just make the time. The family calendar includes serving at the soup kitchen one Sunday morning a month, an hour or two to donate labels, newspapers, and cans to the kids' schools, and individual projects that each is engaged in. Christopher assists the umpire at Little League games once or twice a week, Rena reads to preschoolers every other Saturday afternoon at the neighborhood library, Daniel and Maggie spend an hour visiting elderly at the nursing home, and Max, Barbara, and Jimmy help Gina gather and put together welcome baskets for new members of the community.

Every school year the schedule changes as the kids' interests evolve or new community needs emerge. Following the terrorist attacks on the Pentagon and the World Trade Center, the family went into high gear in terms of fund raising and volunteering. All of the kids, including Jimmy, donated some money to the Salvation Army to help feed the emergency workers, and Gina gave blood at the local hospital. Even Maggie seemed sincerely involved in the effort—I ran into her outside of the grocery store where she was handing out miniature American flags as part of her Youth Group project. At least on that day, patriotism and empathy nudged out self-absorption and Maggie was clearly moved by the need to help others.

I truly believe that this type of parenting—living, modeling, and prioritizing compassion for others—is necessary in our society. We, as parents, need to combat the materialistic, self-centered messages our kids receive *on a daily basis* from friends at school, on the television, and at the malls and movie theaters. I believe that all children are born with the ability to develop empathy and compassion for others, but that ability can be lost if not nurtured by their parents. Most pediatricians will agree with the concept of "contagious crying," even in the hospital nursery. One baby starts in and then a bunch of them begin to wail. Preschool teachers are loaded with stories of how a little one will bump her head and another

Volunteer Yourself

Here are some activities that foster empathy and compassion.

Give up some time for a worthy cause. Work at a homeless shelter or a nursing home. Read to little kids at the library or the pediatric ward at the hospital. Join the Adopt-A-Grandparent program and participate consistently.

Employ your skills. If you like sports, become a referee or an umpire, or perhaps a timekeeper for a kid's sports league. If you're a computer whiz, teach word processing or Web design at an after-school or night class at the recreation center.

Donate money. This is especially good for the kids, as each can contribute some cash on a regular basis to their place of worship or to national organizations such as the American Red Cross, the Salvation Army, or to a local fund for a needy family or ill child.

Have a garage sale. Not only will your family get rid of stuff that's been cluttering up the closets and attic, but the money can be donated to a worthy cause. Get the kids involved, from rounding up old books, toys, and clothes to pricing, stacking, and selling the items.

Sponsor a family. Have each child help to buy or to make a present for the children in the sponsored family at Christmas or for birthdays. Offer food from your family get-togethers and include a nice note expressing your joy that the food will be appreciated by another family.

Become a Big Brother or Big Sister. If time permits, sponsor a kid who doesn't have a mom or a dad consistently in his life.

Join community groups that focus on values development. Boy Scouts and Girl Scouts are great training grounds for children, and parents can become involved as leaders or assistants. Youth groups based at places of worship also encourage volunteerism and compassion, as well as providing companionship and fun for the kids.

will offer a hug or a kiss. The ability to feel empathy is akin to the ability to love—it's quite subjective and perhaps intangible, but it's there. Some folks are born with an innate desire to help others, whereas some, like Maggie and Scott, are not so motivated but can learn the joys of giving by participating in the process. I've come to the conclusion that empathy is not just a *feeling*—it is a *motive* to feel good ourselves. When we help others, we feel better, and I wouldn't be surprised if there is a neurobiological correlation between these feelings of self-enhancement and peace of mind that go hand-in-hand with altruistic behavior.

So try following Gina's and Roger's lead, and begin to promote volunteerism in your own family. There are lots of ways to do it, plenty of needy people and organizations, and there *is* time if you make it a priority!

LIVING THE LAW

Although it may be easier said than done, you can in your own family encourage feelings of empathy, volunteerism, and compassion toward others. It may take some priority changing and creativity, but I've found that it is one of the best, most long-lasting gifts that you can give to your kids as well as to yourself. Have a look at these ideas.

Knock off the excuses. Sure, we're all busy, financially challenged, or stressed out. Try helping others and you may be surprised at how valuable the time spent volunteering is when compared to watching TV or doing a mundane chore. You may even feel better about your own financial situation when you come nose-to-nose with others who have much less than you.

Discuss and define empathy, compassion, and volunteerism. Don't assume that your children will be learning the meaning of these values and behaviors at school or while playing in the neighborhood. It's your job to bring them into your home and to emphasize the importance of giving.

Praise your kids' concern and kindness. Catch them being empathetic and let them know that you see it, appreciate the behavior, and are proud of their efforts. On the other hand, highlight their self-absorbed or egocentric behaviors when they get out of hand, and discuss how that makes you feel.

Take advantage of teachable moments. Whether it's dropping the recyclables at the bins, making sloppy joes at the homeless shelter, or working the concession stand at the ballfields, drag your kids along. Let them participate, if appropriate, and let them see their mom or dad giving back to the community.

Teach emotional consequences. If one of your kids embarrasses another or hurts someone's feelings, discuss how it might affect the other person. Ask your child how they would feel if they were ignored, made fun of, or humiliated. Of course, do this privately so that you are teaching your child and not embarrassing him in the process.

Observe what your child watches. Supervise television and movies as much as possible. Often TV shows and cartoons focus on getting away with bad behavior or humiliating and embarrassing others, or use violence in their presentation. Kids don't need to view this stuff, and it's up to you to stop it or at least to tone it down.

Discuss gratitude. Whenever you can sneak it in, bring up what you and other family members should be grateful for. For example, not every kid has a grandma or a grandpa to hang with. How about living in a neighborhood full of friends to play with? What about the pet that shows unconditional love every day of the year? Talk about a nice teacher that they will never forget or a classmate that made the transition to the new school easier. These are people and things that we tend to take for granted in our busy lives, and a few minutes spent pointing them out can go a long way in raising your child's perception of what's really important.

Stress the don'ts. Try to stay away from stressing competition at the cost of hurting others. Don't overindulge your child—have him earn possessions and privileges in order to appreciate them.

Don't forget the do's. Encourage emotions and sensitivity, and make feelings a natural topic of discussion in your home. Employ role playing when necessary to show your kids how to deal with hurt feelings most appropriately. Encourage apologizing—it lightens the soul.

LAW #15

The Law of Parent versus Child Priorities:

Get on the Same Page

A five-dollar kitchen timer is the most effective, easy, and fabulous way to turn lazy, noncompliant kids into movers and shakers! You've never imagined it could be this easy to get your kids to listen—and act!

Just think, no fussing, no whining, no procrastinating. No nagging. No yelling. No threatening. In a matter of minutes, your whole family will be moving in the same direction.

t's no secret what a kid's number one priority is: to have fun, pure and simple. This makes for a "to do" list highlighted by such critical tasks as watching television, playing video games, hanging out with friends, or biking around the block. Understandably, homework and chores fall much farther down on the list. Mom and Dad, though, clearly have a different set of priorities.

Parents do want their kids to have fun, but they want to balance play with completion of responsibilities. They want the tasks done in a timely manner and don't look forward to the inevitable hassles that go with threatening, barking orders, or generally trying to light a fire under their kids to get them to do their work on time.

It usually comes down to the simple fact that what "now" means to a kid is often different from what "now" means to his folks. Children want chores to be fit in between television shows or a break in playtime. Mom and Dad, however, usually prefer work to be completed before play begins, and that's where the friction starts.

Does this inevitable difference in perception have to become a problem? Not necessarily, especially if you accept that it's a natural part of child rearing because of the differences in parent/child human nature. Just understanding that these differences are normal takes some of the sting out of the issue. Of course your kid would rather play than clean up his bedroom. If you can understand and accept that as typical, then half of the problem is solved. I've found that too many parents get caught up in the emotion of the moment rather than focusing upon problem resolution. My advice is to keep calm and nonchalant and to move on to how you're going to *solve* the problem—quickly, with a minimum of nagging, lecturing, or reminding. Use action or a consequence rather than a lot of yakking, and you'll begin to see your child's behavior change for the better. He may not *want* to clean up the bedroom, but he *will* if there's an effective consequence lurking around the corner.

One of my fondest remembrances is how one family worked on

and resolved this dilemma in their own home. Roz, mother of 9-year-old Abraham, was a stickler for organization, getting things done on time, as well as planning ahead. Sam, her husband of 12 years, was not cut from the same cloth but had found himself living in a home where there was a place for everything and therefore everything needed to be in its place. Instead of just dropping his clothes on the floor at the end of the day, Sam dutifully put them away in drawers or the laundry hamper, and had even become quite a pro at doing the laundry and other household chores himself. Although he felt that Roz's neat-nick ways were a bit much and perhaps unnecessary, Sam stuck with the program since it meant so much to his wife, and he found that it actually was nicer living in a clean and organized environment.

But, to Roz's consternation, Abraham's acorn didn't fall far from his Dad's tree. This kid was a slob by nature, and he saw absolutely no reason to make a bed ("What's the point? I'm just going to unmake it every night!"), pick the stuff up from his bedroom floor ("I know where everything is. I like it like that!"), or put away clean clothes ("What difference does it make where I leave them? If they're on the floor, I can easily see what I have."). Of course, none of these arguments went over well with his mother, and that's when the fun would begin. On a daily basis she was finding herself nagging, reminding, and prodding Abraham to keep his stuff neat and in order. Usually the kid either talked back, ranted indignantly, or just flat-out ignored his mother. If Sam was home during the battles, he often found himself taking sides (with whomever seemed to be making the best argument at the moment) and would inevitably pay for his lack of loyalty by either receiving the cold shoulder from his wife or getting the brushoff from his kid. This was not a particularly happy family when they entered therapy—Roz felt like a drill sergeant to both her husband as well as her son, Sam believed that no matter what side he took he'd never win, and Abraham felt that his mom was ridiculous and on the way to losing it.

At our first session, I explained to the family that it's typical for parental priorities, time pressures, and schedules to clash with children's preferences. From the child's reference point, experience, and interests, a messy bedroom is often a benchmark for how much stuff one owns—not a sign of disorganization or of being a slob. Wasting energy on making a bed intrudes upon valuable time and resources that could be allotted to skateboarding or watching television. Putting away clothes in drawers or hanging them up in closets may not only be wasted effort, but out of sight is, well, out of mind. It's difficult to inventory what you have when it's not directly in the line of view!

So how to best set up the formula for getting things done correctly, with minimal hassle, and, most importantly, within the parent's time frame—and without too much kid fussing? As I explained to Roz and Sam, it's simple—buy a timer and use it. (I can't tell you the number of clients who have told me that had they known of and used my *timer technique* that they probably could have solved many problems without formal counseling.) Why is this technique so effective? Because timers and buzzers turn gray areas into black and white—no ambiguity allowed. A buzzer turns *now* into 1, 5, or 10 minutes—not when the next commercial break occurs. And as you've probably learned from your own kids, just give a child some ambiguity or a shade of gray, and you're a sitting duck for an argument or a problem!

I informed Sam that for the program to work best, he'd need to be on the same page of the book with his wife. When either parent wanted something to be accomplished, they were to ask Abraham to do it within a certain time frame. That could be "before your sitcom begins," "after dinner and before you begin to use any electricity," or better yet, "before the timer buzzes." If the kid began to argue, they were to ignore his complaints, set the timer, and walk away. If he accomplished the task on time, reasonably correctly, and without a bunch of grumping and griping, life would move on. If he didn't, then he would lose out on a privilege or receive a "bad point" or other negative consequence. No ifs, ands, or buts . . . just a consequence for not doing as told when told.

Sure, Abraham, upon hearing my suggestions, was less than thrilled with the idea, but it ended up being more fair and pleasant in the long run. Roz, over the next few weeks, began to pick her battles, and Sam found the buzzer to be a "safe" mechanism to use with his kid. He was no longer in the middle trying to choose sides between his wife and his son, and Sam quickly saw how pleasant a home can be when the petty arguments disappear. Abraham resigned himself to picking up his dirty laundry on a daily basis and found that he had even more time to skateboard or watch TV as his mom was no longer lecturing him about responsibility and organization on a daily basis.

So if you want to get your kids to get moving and to accept *your* definition of what *now* is, consider establishing the rule that the "buzzer has to be beat" or they will receive a negative consequence. Or for kids who have trouble prioritizing their time outside of the house, make the rule that the child cannot go out to play without wearing a watch with the alarm set. In addition, you can use the timer for motivating your kids to clean up their bedrooms, get the mail from the mailbox, or come in for dinner without having to be hassled, nagged, or reminded five times. It works, folks, and it will save you big bucks in therapy fees!

Keep in mind that differences in priorities between parent and child grow even more complex as the years go on. Many folks I speak with take it very personally when their children have different viewpoints on the world and how they perceive what is and isn't important. Often parents believe that either they've been remiss in their child-rearing practices or that there is something wrong with the kid. Well, usually it's neither—we're just dealing with different people who may see the world via different priorities. Neither take on life is necessarily better. So don't expect that your child is going to be a clone of you, with all the same opinions and points of view. Do what you can to engage them in conversation. Teach them, persuade them, and most of all, lead them. But remember they must—and will—make their own decisions about what's important in their lives.

But until then, get that timer going!

LIVING THE LAW

How to begin to change the priorities in your house? Well, try the following suggestions.

Call a family meeting. Explain to the kids your frustration with responses such as "in a minute," "I don't want to," or "it's not my turn" when you request something of them. Discuss how before-school dawdling gets everyone stressed out and begins the day on the wrong foot. Remind them of how, just that morning, you spent 25 minutes yelling, nagging, and hassling them to get ready, and when they were finally leaving, you gave each a kiss and said, "Have a nice day!" Now what's wrong with this picture? Personally, I'd have a heck of a time having a nice day after having been screamed at for almost half an hour!

Ask for their suggestions and solutions. Be sure to listen without interrupting. Someone just may offer a brilliant idea that may work, but don't count on that always happening. Most likely the kids will complain about "not being morning people" and how it's somehow your fault that they have to get up so early for school. Ignore this stuff—don't even bother to go there.

Discuss general time limits. Start your list by working from morning through evening until bedtime, noting each chore or responsibility that needs to be done on a daily basis. Most days will mandate similar activities, although weekend responsibilities may be different than weekday chores, and time pressures may be lessened on Saturdays and Sundays. After you've decided as a family what needs to be completed, and in what order, begin to determine how much time should be allowed for task completion. Don't be surprised if this feels like you're negotiating a legal contract—it is an agreement of sorts, with all parties present in your family's mediation exercise.

Set reasonable time limits for each task. Take the individual child's personality, nature, and state of the mess in their bedroom into consideration. Your neat-freak daughter may need only a few minutes per day to pick up her shoes and socks in her bedroom, but your laissez-faire son may need 15 to 20 minutes of work to get his room under control. Be prepared for the kids to begin negotiations by requesting longer time limits than you feel comfortable with—listen, determine if it can be fit into your day, and then accept the time frame or lower it to fit the reality of your family's responsibilities.

Make exceptions when necessary—and explain why. For instance, if one of your children has a bunch of kids over for the afternoon, the time allowed to pick up the playroom or bedroom may need to be doubled. Or, if time is going to be devoted to a school project all evening, then the bathroom clean-up or dishwasher duty may be excused for the evening. This allows your children to see that you are trying to be reasonable and flexible when there is good reason, but that you are intending to stay within the system, and you continue to expect things to be done on time.

Present each child with their own timer. The buzzer is theirs to use to help them to move faster in terms of getting out of bed on time, bathing, brushing teeth, completing homework, and anything else that needs some putting the pedal to the metal. Show them the *Mom or Dad timer* also and explain that you'll be simultaneously setting yours so that they won't be able to stop their timers in order to give themselves more leeway. In discussing this, don't worry that you're putting a sneaky idea in their heads—most kids figure it out the first day on the timer system.

Review the program. Summarize what will be timed and what will not, as well as stating the consequences attached to not beating the buzzer. I suggest loss of television privileges in the evening if the kid didn't beat the homework buzzer earlier in the day or no dessert if the child dawdled too much and didn't come to the dinner table in a timely manner. Be creative and think outside of the box—use what works with the individual child.

Use it or lose it. Many of my clients fastidiously use the timer system for the first month or two and are awed at the new, compliant children who are now residing in their homes. Then the folks get lazy. The timer becomes misplaced in a drawer, and trust me, the kids notice that it's no longer being used. If they see that you are not on top of timing the problem areas in the day—watch out! Some children will continue to respect your priorities, while others will begin to slack off. If you see this insidious process occurring, it's time to rifle through the kitchen drawers, find the buzzers, and resurrect the timer system. There may be a few grumps and groans from the kids, but it will work again and you'll be a happier, less frustrated parent.

The Law of Communication:

Shut Up and Listen

Here's how to set the stage for good communication, even if your kid seems to prefer to grunt rather than to converse. Watch for communication pitfalls, don't be a *fixer*—be an effective listener. This method helps your child open up and helps you avoid the most common mistakes of parent-child communication. And remember, once the communication with your child improves, all things are possible.

Have a kid living under your roof who seems unwilling or unable to tell you his concerns, worries, or even the daily goings-on? Well, join the pack of moms and dads who feel that they just can't seem to break into their kids' hearts and heads no matter what they try. And to make the situation even more puzzling, you may even have another child in the same house who babbles constantly about her feelings, what you've done to mess up her life, or the details of her friends' daily activities. Sometimes you wish that your budding talk show guest's chatter would somehow rub off on her more reticent brother!

Well, both styles can be fine, but each comes with pros and cons. You're never quite sure how to react when your talkative one has a meltdown—is she really in a state of crisis or will she recover before dinnertime? But at least your daughter keeps you informed of her daily ups and downs so you can keep a finger on her emotional barometer. What about her brother, the kid who rarely shares his feelings and at times seems to have none, even when you know that his heart has been broken or his pride hurt? That's tough and it takes some savvy parenting to help the reticent communicator to open up.

Setting the Stage

There are some basic do's and don'ts for encouraging your kids to communicate with you. Set the stage for gaining your child's trust in confiding in you as early as possible. Habits begun at a young age are easier to form and have greater staying power. Try not to be critical when your child complains to you about a problem. If your initial impulse is to blame your son ("And what did you do to provoke Michael to hit you?"), he'll most likely think twice before sharing his problems with you again in the near future. Making assumptions like this can be off base and damaging to a relationship. Gather the facts before jumping to conclusions. By listening first, you're telling your child that you are on the same team and that you're there for him, although you may not always agree with his thoughts or actions.

Schedule time together. To encourage your kid to use you as a sounding board or a confidant, you need to have consistent private time with each other. I've found with my own kids that bedtime lends itself to introspection. It's a time to wrap up the day, both emotionally and physically, and if your evening routine contains this ritual, it becomes second nature to use it as talking time. I've also learned about my kids' feelings (sometimes more than I've wanted to) by taking walks with them. Strolling around the neighborhood can lead to quiet moments, mindless "weather talk," and even occasionally, shared confidences. Looking back, I wouldn't replace those moments with anything. So set up a routine that periodically places you alone with each child, be it driving to ballet or football, bedtime tuck-ins, or pounding the pavement together. You'll be pleased with how quickly the silence is broken and thoughts and confidences are shared!

Be especially sensitive during times when your child searches you out to talk. Even if your kids have the uncanny knack of uncorking their emotions in the middle of your important phone calls, take the time to listen. I know that it may be inconvenient to break from your thoughts or work in order to pay attention, but if you don't take advantage of the moment, you may not have it again.

Shut up and listen. Okay, now that you've set the stage for communication, *you* need to become a good listener if you want your children to confide in you. When it comes to kids' feelings, most of us have a tendency to jump in and try to fix things so that they are not uncomfortable, in emotional pain, or worried. When you rush to the rescue, though, your actions may be perceived by your child as, "I can't figure this out, so Mom has to do it," or "I shouldn't have to experience indecision or confusion. Dad's going to fix it." Wrong messages, folks—although your intentions are noble, you are depriving your child of learning how to deal with negative emotions or remedying the situation himself. Also, rushing in with a quick fix can be interpreted as trying to talk kids out of their true feelings, "You're overreacting— Jamie really didn't mean it that way!" Whether Jamie meant to hurt your child's feelings is not the issue—your kid's feelings *are* hurt, and that is what needs to be dealt with.

Once you've listened, help your child to accurately label his emotions. Most of us are adept at using psychological defense mechanisms to shield us from discomfort. For example, your son may come home from school and slam the door on his way to the bedroom. When you try to speak with him, he either grunts loudly or ignores you, or perhaps yells that he's madder than a hornet. However, what may really be happening is that he's embarrassed about missing an easy foul shot that could have clinched the game for his basketball team. Is he really angry? Yep, but the more basic emotions are humiliation, embarrassment, and fear that he won't be a starter in tomorrow's game. Help him to sort out the difference between his surface feelings (anger and frustration) and those at the core of the problem (concern over what his coach and teammates feel about him). Helping your child to label and interpret emotions will ensure that he's working on the true problem.

Now that you've listened and labeled, it's time for problem resolution. Notice that I didn't say "problem solving," as there may not be an acceptable solution for every predicament. Sometimes kids just have to learn to accept frustration and to move on, and at other times they'll learn to agree to disagree. Start by letting your child know that her feelings are normal. In fact, you may remember feeling the same way yourself when it seemed that the entire class was invited to a birthday party and you were left out. Reflecting, or mirroring, your child's feelings will validate that it's okay to feel hurt, angry, or left out when you've been snubbed or rejected by others.

Help your child to develop options and alternatives for handling the problem situation—jumpstart the creative process by sharing an idea or two. However, giving a list of 10 possible responses that your teenage daughter can use to heal a rift with her friends is inappropriate—one or two should grease the wheel. Let her do the rest of the idea-producing, otherwise she'll forever be dependent upon you or others for generating solutions.

Ensure future communication. I teach two techniques to my clients that go a long way toward cementing their children's trust in communication. First, parents should *clarify* that even if the confidence shared is a 'fessing up to an inappropriate behavior (breaking a vase, sneaking out at night, using the phone when grounded), that they are proud of their child for telling the truth. Let your kid know that you respect her courage for coming clean, and even though there may be a consequence for the misdeed, it will certainly be less than if you had found out about it on your own!

Be a good confidant yourself. When your child tells you a secret or shares feelings that are touchy, keep it to yourself. Don't be a gossip and let slip your son's crush on the gal sitting next to him in geometry class or your daughter's dream to be an astronaut. If the child asks you to keep the information to yourself, that's exactly what you must do, no matter how cute it is or how much Grandma would be tickled. Trust is too easily broken and so tough to attain. Getting your kids to confide in you is tricky business, but if you are sensitive and patient, they'll learn to trust your heart and your judgment!

LIVING THE LAW

Promote communication. Tell your children that you enjoy hearing what's going on in their lives and that you feel that it's important to establish good communication within the home.

Be especially sensitive with reticent kids. If your child tends to keep things to herself, assure her that you can keep a secret, especially if she tells you that it's a sensitive topic. If so, keep your word and keep your mouth zipped!

Don't jump in to fix problems. Many times children just need to air their feelings or to vent frustrations—they don't necessarily want your advice. Often, only time will fix it, but while your child is waiting, it may help to vent, to get some emotional validation, or to just touch base with a parent about feelings, both negative and positive.

Model good communication skills yourself. Tell your children about some of your problems—but be selective. Perhaps discuss your frustration about an annoying coworker or a difficult decision that you're going to have to make in the near future. Let them see that gathering other people's opinions and ideas may be very helpful and can enable you to better put things into perspective. Hopefully they'll see the connection to sharing their own problems and decisions with you.

Set the stage. Try to have some alone time with each of the children every day. Take their individual natures into account—some like to talk in the morning on the way to school, whereas others are more relaxed and communicative at night, just before bedtime.

Make sure that one child doesn't consistently communicate for the other. The more verbal kid needs to learn to respect the quieter child's reticence and to be patient and tolerant with the challenges he may feel in terms of communication. Applaud your talkative one's concern, but ask that she allow her sibling to do his own communicating.

Promote good listening skills in your kids. If your child is very verbal and communicates feelings readily, help her to be a good listener. Teach that it's better to let others finish their sentences and thoughts, to shy away from being too judgmental, and to learn to keep confidences if they want to become good confidants themselves!

LAW #17

The Law of Multiple Perceptions:

Don't Reason with the Unreasonable

One of the most important rules of kid human nature is that they can be flat-out unreasonable, and then blame you for not automatically seeing it their way. Don't take it personally; in fact, you don't have to take it at all! Set your rules, feel guilty about it if you must, but take a stand and don't budge from what you know to be right for your kid.

One of us has to go" was Stacey's comment as she and her 16-year-old son, Peter, settled into my office. As a single mom, she enjoyed the ability to call the shots with her kid, but she definitely didn't like the responsibility of having to constantly wear the black hat. Apparently, Peter, as he grew older, wanted greater privileges and freedoms but was less than thrilled with the increased responsibilities and consequences. Lately he had been on a campaign to prove to his mother that as a high school junior he should be allowed to choose his activities and run his own life. As Peter put it, "Every one of my friends has no curfew and they can go to parties even if the parents aren't home." I counseled Stacey that if that was true, her son had no business hanging around with a bunch of unsupervised thugs. Most likely, though, Peter was exaggerating their freedoms a bit.

His current onslaught centered upon trying to convince his mom to let him spend the weekend with a friend, one whose folks were scheduled to be out of town during the stay. Peter and Stacey were close to fisticuffs over this issue and wanted me to act as mediator in deciding what he should be allowed to do. Should Stacey permit her 16-year-old to spend the weekend with a friend in an unsupervised situation? Absolutely not! You'd have to be nuts to leave two teenage boys alone for a few days. Stacey knew that, but why couldn't Peter see it? I asked Stacey what she thought would happen if I lined up 100 parents in my office and asked them if they'd give permission to their own children. I informed her that most, if not all, would look at me as if I were loopy and irresponsible for even asking and would respond with a resounding, "No way!" So why do Stacey and I have one perception of the request (crazy) and Peter has such a different perception (fine idea)?

It's because he's 16 and immature, a place where Stacey and I haven't been in quite a while. What we perceive as sensible may be seen as nonsense to a teenager, and vice versa. From Peter's point of view, the parent-free weekend sounded like a great idea—hey, two guys can take care of themselves and what if a few friends just happen to stop

135

by? No big deal—they could handle it. From the teen's point of view, our concerns were frivolous. On the other hand, Stacey and I knew from experience that a few kids without adult supervision is a recipe for disaster. Even if their intentions are noble, things could quickly get out of hand. Many a party has occurred by spontaneous combustion—one kid mentioning to another that the folks would be gone and before you know it the little get-together has blossomed into a full-fledged free-for-all. Anxious or annoyed neighbors may call the police, and kids who didn't plan to get into trouble are now in over their heads. Stacey noted that she had witnessed this firsthand as a teen herself and therefore was cautious about letting Peter flirt with trouble.

But talk as we may, Peter wasn't buying into our logic. That's because you just can't reason with the unreasonable. From the kid's point of view, his mom and I were being overprotective, supercautious fuddy-duddies who probably never partied in our lives. This wasn't the time or place for Stacey or me to argue that point with Peter. My goal was to teach Stacey the concept of not trying to reason with the unreasonable. And she also needed to grow a spine, a sturdy backbone that would help her stand up to her cantankerous son in the future.

When Kids Just Don't Get It

The fact was that Peter didn't get it because Peter didn't want to get it. Sure, he felt he was capable of keeping the weekend at his friend's house down to a dull roar, but he didn't want to think of what could happen if the football team showed up and a few kids landed in the slammer for underage drinking, vandalism, or trespassing upon the neighbors' property. Peter preferred to dwell upon how much fun a parent-free weekend would be. All of our reasoning, cajoling, and fact presentation didn't seem to make a dent in this thick-headed teen!

So Stacey had to make a unilateral decision. She really didn't want to let Peter stay in an unsupervised situation, but as a single parent she didn't have anyone to pass the "No, you can't do it buck" to. Upon my suggestion, Stacey listened to Peter and together they made a list of the pros and cons of the proposed adventure at his buddy's house. It went something like this.

Pro:
- No folks telling us what to do
- Eating whenever and whatever we want
- Having friends over at will
- No folks telling us what to do
- Cleaning up right before the parents return, but not on a daily basis
- Sleeping in
- Watching television and renting videos
- No folks telling us what to do

Con:
- The whole high school stopping by and an instant party emerging and getting out of hand
- Something getting broken
- Something getting stolen
- Drugs on the scene
- Potential arrests
- Peter getting grounded for life

Following that exercise, Peter was still grumpy but had realized that the free-for-all may just not be worth it. He eventually acquiesced and invited his friend to spend the weekend at his home. Stacey allowed the guys to have a few buddies over, and Peter did have a great weekend in spite of the disagreement with his mom.

However, had he not seen the light and compromised with his mother, I would have advised her to just say "no." The message is this: At times there may be no reasoning with the unreasonable. Parents must call the shots and if the kid is angry, so be it. You are not there to be his buddy—he can find plenty of friends at school or in the neighborhood. You are there to be his mentor and supporter, and to set limits on his behavior. You should try to offer reasonable solutions, and to use techniques such as the pro/con list that Stacey and Peter employed.

To be fair, you do want to try and understand his perception of the situation. Make sure that you've listened well to your kid's request, considered it fully, and determined that your response is reasonable. If it is, stick to it, but don't expect him to be happy with your answer. He may really believe that you're the unreasonable one for not seeing things his way.

But to try to make him see the world as you do is a waste of time—so when the horse is dead, realize that it's time to get off! Once you're sure that he has heard your side of the issue and that your mind is made up, move on. Let your child stew for as long as it takes, but don't keep banging your head against the wall trying to convince him that you're right and he's wrong. Remember, from a 16-year-old's viewpoint, you may be wrong, unfair, or just plain stodgy and out of touch. To expect your child to reason as you do would be to ignore the differences in your age, experience, and wisdom.

LIVING THE LAW

Understand kid human nature. This is what makes kids so unreasonable—what kids don't know is often significantly more important, greater in scope, and more meaningful than what they do understand. The problem is that many children think that they know it all and that the bill of goods you're trying to sell them is just some parenting plot to make life easier for you and more miserable for them. That's part of normal kid human nature.

Realize that they're just kids. Don't be surprised when your years of wisdom, mistakes, and experience fall upon deaf ears. It takes a while to get through thick heads and defensive attitudes. And some kids just seem to have to experience the pain before they begin to understand and finally get it.

Don't get angry. Since you now understand kid human nature, you should no longer be getting so irritated and can begin to understand why your idea of sense may be perceived as nonsense to your child. There's no point in getting frustrated with kid self-absorption, lack of common sense, or a seeming inability to learn from experience or lecture. You can't change this.

Sit the kid down. Listen to his desires and see if a compromise can be reached, as in Peter's case when his friend spent the weekend at his house.

When the horse is dead, get off. If you've tried reasoning and your kid is still irrational or has a bad case of the attitudes, just move on. Set your rule, whether it's saying no to a sleepover at a beer-drinking bash, riding a scooter in the street without a helmet, or your daughter wearing lipstick in second grade. If it isn't reasonable within your family's code of values, then it isn't going to happen.

Become a benevolent dictator. If you can't come to a comfortable compromise, then revert to Law #4, take on the benevolent dictator role, and cast the final vote!

LAW #18

The Law of
the Praise Junkie:

Make Praise
Appropriate,
Not Addictive

Praise is like frosting on a cake. A little makes it taste better and too much will ruin everything. Kids need your encouragement and love it when you recognize their accomplishments. Just don't ruin their trust by leading them to believe every little thing they do is worthy of adoration and a chorus of cheers. When they find out otherwise, they'll be crushed and probably blame you for making them so needy of approval.

Recently, I had the opportunity to observe one of my families, 5-year-old Joshua and his parents, in action. They had arrived at my office about 15 minutes early, and having returned from lunch with a few minutes to spare, I was chatting with my secretary in the waiting room. As I was gathering my things to walk back to my private office, I was taken aback by a series of Joshua's mother's comments. The kid was playing with some blocks on the floor, and Mom was emitting a running commentary on his progress. "Oh, Joshua, that's such a nice stack of blocks. You are so smart," followed by "What a great job. I couldn't have built that when I was your age." Then Dad added to the drivel with some that's-my-boy, chip-off-the-old-block statements that nearly caused my secretary to gag. After all, the kid was 5 years old, and stacking up a few wooden blocks is not a great achievement. You would have thought that Joshua had discovered a cure for the common cold by the way his folks were carrying on. No wonder he was having problems following directions in kindergarten—no teacher would be able to give him the amount of attention and praise necessary to keep the child motivated.

What is wrong with praising a child? Actually, a lot if it's given inappropriately. Most of us have evolved as parents believing that giving praise is like eating calorie-free chocolate—the more the better. But new research suggests that complimenting children in certain ways may set them up to become *praise junkies*—looking to their parents or others for validation of almost every act or feeling, rather than developing an internal barometer for self-esteem and feelings of accomplishment and achievement.

Recent psychological study findings are quite straightforward and to the point—kids need praise to guide the development of such characteristics as self-control, self-discipline, frustration tolerance, and perseverance. But studies recently completed through the Department of Psychology at Columbia University in New York City note that the *manner* in which children are praised as well as *what* they are praised for makes a significant difference in how they later fare when faced with challenges or perceived failures.

The results suggest that kids who are praised for effort and hard work begin to value learning opportunities, whereas children who are praised for their abilities value performance. The studies showed that praising a child for a personal characteristic such as intelligence ("Aren't you smart. I can count on you for getting an A on your reports!") can often backfire. The researchers noted that kids given praise that evaluates the child or their traits and abilities (known as *person praise*) were significantly more likely to display helpless reactions (cognitions, affects, and behaviors) when they were later challenged with more difficult tasks than children who received *effort* or *strategy praise* ("Wow, I like the way you looked at this problem from several angles and chose an unusual solution").

What that means, folks, is that kids who are praised for self (traits such as physical attractiveness, intelligence, or possessions) are prone to deal less well in the future with problems and challenges than are children who are complimented for their work effort, regardless of prior success. In a nutshell, when you compliment work effort, you often help lead your child to a solid work ethic that will continue to develop as he grows to and through adulthood. The time-worn sayings "It's not whether you win or lose that's important, it's how you play the game," or "Success is more perspiration than inspiration," apparently are not just Great-Grandma's ramblings—there's now clinical data to back her up!

When parents express appreciation for what a child has accomplished by focusing on the effort put in or the method used to accomplish the task, rather than by labeling or evaluating the child as a whole, this sets the stage for perseverance in the later years. Praise for the effort, strategizing, work, and persistence children put into their accomplishments more fully recognizes their achievements than does ability praise. This means that kids should be praised for *how* they do their work rather than for the final product or their IQ score.

This is actually easier to accomplish than you might think at first glance. "Trying and failing" occurs more often in children's lives than do large successes. Think of all of the times that your kid takes the basketball onto the driveway and tries to shoot hoops. That 10-foot height can be daunting to a 10-year-old who comes in at about 4 feet 4 inches, yet somehow he keeps trying. And trying, and trying. And then one day it finally happens—whether it was the wind lending a hand or some skill and strength actually kicking in, the kid swooshes the ball through the net. He's thrilled, and I'm sure that you'll be the first to hear about it and to praise his accomplishment. But consider all of the attempts at making a basket that preceded that first success. Sure, giving him an "atta-boy" for making the shot is nice, but it's your consistent praise and attention noting his daily, unsuccessful efforts that really teach him perseverance. Most kids with skill and strength can make a basket and continue to practice, but it takes someone very special to face defeat and carry on, failed shot after failed shot. Let him know the difference.

It's also emotionally risky to get back in the saddle after failure. Friends may tease your child and wear down his motivation. But your support praises the process, not the child, and serves not only as encouragement but turns the focus onto effort, rather than success. As you may know from your own career, we cannot always control the outcome of every situation we're in, but we sure can steer our energies in the proper direction. Yet we can do this only if we've been trained to continue without immediate success and to view obstacles as challenges, not as annoying or impossible problems interfering with our lives.

Whether it's shooting hoops in the driveway, taking an advanced placement course in high school rather than an average class, or trying out for a sports team already populated with talented athletes, your kid will be much more inclined toward challenges and positive risk-taking if he has been raised with a steady diet of process or effort praise, rather than being adulated for his IQ or strong muscles.

Try to remember this if your 4-year-old daughter just can't keep her crayon between the lines but she's trying her best, or your 16-year-old son is giving it his all but still scares the dickens out of you when you take him out driving those first few times. Remind yourself that it's the effort that counts, not today's performance. In fact, there's another body of research suggesting that when things come too easily, it's human nature to be unappreciative, take our abilities for granted and not be able to rise to the occasion when we are unexpectedly challenged by adversity.

LIVING THE LAW

Here's the scoop to avoid raising a praise junkie.

Praise the process rather than the person. Do say "Stacking blocks is tough for a little guy like you, let's keep trying," rather than "You're so smart. Stacking blocks will be a piece of cake!"

Be specific. Praise so that your kids will understand exactly what behaviors you are complimenting. Say, "That was a tough math problem and I saw that you were becoming frustrated. But you stuck with it," rather than, "Good job on your math homework."

Praise often, but don't overdo it. Too much praise tends to water down the effectiveness and purpose of complimenting. (I can't tell you how many children and teenagers have noted to me that they are skeptical of their parents' praise because, "It's just my Mom saying I'm pretty. She has to say that because she's my mother.") If you want your kids to trust and to believe in you, then you have to be believable.

Love unconditionally, but praise conditionally. No matter what your kids do, I'm sure that they are well loved. However, they don't need to be enveloped with compliments 24/7—it's too much for them to absorb and to believe, as well as too draining for you. You can be an effective parent if you praise only when it's deserved. Our children will develop their self-concept largely from how the real world treats them. And in my experience, most of us are respected for our work ethic, not just for showing up or for what we possess.

With older children, you may have to look for, and take advantage of, opportunities to compliment. As little ones there are so many "firsts" (sitting up, crawling, walking, talking) that it's a literal praise-a-thon. However, as they mature, many kids tend to communicate more with their friends than with you, and you may not even be aware of some of their efforts or accomplishments. Therefore, a good place to start with the middle and high schoolers is to discuss projects and schoolwork. Also, athletic activities can be fertile ground for effort praise, even if the kid doesn't lead the league in homers or field goals. As long as he's out there giving it his all—that's what is deserving of your compliments and reinforcement.

LAW

The Law of Appropriateness:

Grow the Rules with Your Child

As kids grow, often so do their problem behaviors. What's cute at three just doesn't cut it at six. Growing up can be a good news/bad news process—with each developmental stage come new skills and awareness, as well as new behavioral challenges! From bad language to risk-taking to tattoos, here are some strategies to keep the kids on track at any age.

n over 20 years of experience as a mom and a psychologist, I've found that kids have the most difficulties when they are undergoing intense physical, social, or cognitive development. What may appear to be bad behavior at these ages may really be experimental behavior, ranging from trying out new activities to developing novel ideas or attitudes.

There is good news and bad news at each stage, so parents need to understand what's really cooking with their kids during these times. Each child goes through these episodes in different ways at different times. But no matter when or how your child hits these "touchy spots," you can manage their behavior better if you understand what your kid is going through. Let's start by having a look at the little ones.

Preschool

Good news: Increased verbal skills. **Bad news:** Talks back.

At this age children are mastering words and can express their needs fairly clearly. But by becoming more verbal they also begin to talk back. Preschoolers are able to not only say "no" in a demanding tone but may actually yell at you or become argumentative. It's not that your little angel has suddenly donned a set of devil's horns, but he has begun to develop a mind of his own. He may not see the need to leave the sandbox and come in for lunch, and may let you have it right between the eyes. "You're not the boss of me!" was one of my own kid's personal favorites, and I learned a long time ago to be the big guy and to not take the bait. I knew that I had to be the boss, but getting in the kid's face every time that he said it just wasn't necessary. And to take these talkbacks personally would be a losing proposition!

You should:

- Have a sense of humor.

- Keep comments in perspective.

- Know that you are (or should be) the boss, and don't flaunt it.

- Expect some talking back—correct it when necessary, model polite behavior yourself, and move on!

Good news: Better gross and fine motor control. **Bad news:** High risk behaviors.

Preschoolers begin to learn new skills such as swimming or riding a bike with training wheels. However, these successes often lead to a false sense of security and you may see your little one engage in risky behavior such as climbing trees or jumping down from a top step. This is normal but can cause tension between you and your child as he explores his world—and you, the parent, must watch out for his safety.

You should:

- Know your child's style—is she an impulsive risk-taker or a cautious observer? If it's the former, keep a set of eyes on her constantly. Secure swimming pool entrances, add front door locks out of her reach, and try to look at the world from her perspective. If a chair is good for climbing, wouldn't two chairs stacked on top of each other be an even better idea?

- Know your style—are you a Nervous Nellie, afraid to let your little one explore even the safest of playgrounds? If so, back off a notch—keep your eyes on the kid but allow him to run, jump, and explore his world within reason.

- If your styles clash and you feel that you are either overfocused on child safety or perhaps too laissez-faire, consider having your partner or childcare provider take over at the playground or block party. What's important is that a balance is met between your youngster's risk-taking behavior and ability to explore his world.

Grade School

Good news: Gains confidence. **Bad news:** Becomes bossy.

By 5 or 6 years of age most children have entered school and gained confidence in their abilities. They have acquired many skills in a short amount of time and are now ready to start showing them off. This newfound confidence can develop into bossy behavior and your child may come across to others as a know-it-all.

You should:

- Encourage high self-esteem but also let your kid know that it's most effective to teach others in a gentle and caring way.

- If your kid tends to employ the "bulldozer technique"—pushing his ideas upon others without their permission or interest—explain how annoying that can be to peers as well as to adults.

- Model or role-play effective communication skills with your grade schooler; include listening skills as well as talking in your conversation.

Middle School

Good news: Develops sense of self. **Bad news:** Becomes moody.

Uh-oh, the tween years! Those hormones have begun to kick in and sometimes it seems as if they have possessed your child. Tweens are discovering who they are as individuals, which is a wonderful thing, but they can also be extremely moody, displaying abrupt emotional changes as well as outbursts. Some of this behavior can be blamed on hormones. Understanding this is not an excuse for inappropriate behavior, but it will help you to be more sensitive to what your child is going through and may allow you to get to the root of a problem instead of merely focusing on the symptom.

You should:

- Stop and think before talking or suggesting advice. If your daughter is rude and acts withdrawn, perhaps she needs a few minutes to put her thoughts in order.

- Be patient. It may take the kid a while to stop the rumination and to slink out of her self-absorption long enough to tell you what's up.

- Expect her not to think like an adult. She's a kid and lives in a world of popularity, peer pressure, and stick-thin models on the covers of magazines. Of course her self-esteem (and therefore judgment) will be shaky—expect it, understand it, and try not to be too judgmental yourself.

- Remember, please, what life was like for you as a tween!

High School

Good news: Feels independent. **Bad news:** Thinks he is invincible.

Many teenagers think they know everything. It's typical of adolescence, as teens begin to feel independent and self-sufficient. Perhaps they have an after-school job and are earning extra cash. Some have a driver's license and can get themselves where they need to go. With increasing independence, though, comes the precarious belief that they are invincible, immortal, or unstoppable.

This is a time when balance is key. Giving your teen some freedom to make choices is important while he is still living with you and you can be a guide. Try to keep the lines of communication open. Establish appropriate rules, but don't be so strict that he wants to run from you. Understand that this stage represents huge developmental strides and therefore some limit pushing is bound to occur.

Even though your child may try your patience, remember that "this too shall pass." Your kid doesn't have it in for you. In most cases, they're hoping that you'll help them and will try to understand your guidance.

You should:

- Have a sense of humor and don't take every comment or mood as representative of your child's true feelings or permanent attitude.

- For every limit-setting behavior that you impose, try to offer a positive action in response. Provide her with a model to copy via your own actions or reactions.

- If you are concerned about toning down typical teenage self-absorbed behavior, teach your kid how to be more sensitive to others. You cannot expect your child to fill in the void with a positive behavior on her own. Your acts of altruism will go a long way in teaching her how to give to others without focusing upon "What's in it for me?"

Using the Laws with Specific Developmental Problems

As you've seen, kids can be especially tough to deal with during times of intense change. I'd like to present a "sampler" of how to deal with specific behavior problems from a developmental standpoint. You may or may not have the joy of experiencing these particular issues, but just in case, here's how I'd handle them using the laws provided in this book. These are typical of the ages that they represent, and although your own children may have other quirky behaviors, the techniques used can be extrapolated to other problem areas.

Biting: Stop the Chomp

Problem: Having your toddler or preschooler clamp down on the forearm of your best friend's son is not only frightening, but it's really embarrassing. What kind of parent raises a kid who bites his buddies? Well, just about any parent, as this type of behavior is not as rare as you may think. Many little ones go through a biting phase in their early development. Most biters seem to outgrow this behavior when they can use words to express their needs and feelings, rather than depending upon their teeth to get the job done.

Resolution: It's important to teach children that biting really hurts. But please don't bite back just to get your message across! The most common parental reaction to being bitten is to bite or to smack the child. Although retaliation will definitely get your kid's attention, the wrong lesson may be taught. There are more civil and effective ways of letting your child know that biting is inappropriate. First, respond with a firm "no" as you remove the child's mouth from your body part. Keep your verbalization short and simple. "Don't bite me. That hurts and you are not allowed to do that!" should clearly get the message across. I suggest to my clients that the "no" must be said firmly and that close eye contact is established. This usually makes the perpetrator think twice before clamping down on your fingers again!

If you're dealing with a dyed-in-the-wool biter and this approach is less than effective, further consequences are in order. Try placing the child for a timeout in a chair, on the bottom step, in a corner, or a safe but boring spot. Kids generally dislike isolation and the timeout experience should reinforce that biting results in less parental or teacher attention, not more.

Probably the best way to deal with biting behavior, though, is to prevent it from happening in the first place. Try to determine if there is a pattern to your son's biting. In what situations does it occur most often—at school or home, when tired or wired, with close pals or only with new kids? Many children bite when over-stimulated, and you may find that a few minutes of quiet solitary play will give your son back the self-control necessary to play with others more appropriately.

In addition to considering restricting your son's environment while he's going through the biting phase, it's also wise to teach him some pro-social actions. After saying no to aggression, follow up with a behavioral suggestion such as "I know that you want to play with Jason's blocks. Let's ask him if you can and if not, we'll play with the cars." Repeatedly showing your child an alternative technique for getting his needs met will eventually teach him to use his words rather than his teeth or other aggressive maneuvers. It may not work overnight, but it will be effective eventually. Kids can be stubborn and ornery and may need several go-rounds before they get the message.

Not to fear, though. Your child's biting behavior, although embarrassing and perhaps nonsensical, will pass. Biting is not so much a predictor of future behavior problems as it is descriptive of emotional immaturity. Help your child to get through this stage of development by providing close supervision, removal from overstimulating situations, and a firm "no" or negative consequence such as a timeout or loss of a privilege. Don't worry—he won't bite his third-grade teacher when frustrated—that would not be cool!

Offensive Language: Where Did You Get That Mouth?

Problem: Nasty language is a fact of life—almost all children go through a phase of emitting inappropriate words at one or more stages of development. There are three phases of using bad language that many children go through: around the second birthday (during early language acquisition), beginning in late preschool (at 4 or 5 years of age and progressing into grade school), and during the teen years. Using offensive language is a normal, yet embarrassing, activity that is easier to curb the younger the offender.

Resolution for preschoolers: Generally, little kids use profanity or bad language in imitation of a parent or an older sibling. At this young age most kids are in the phase of language acquisition, where mimicry is a common occurrence. You may feel proud when your daughter finally puts three words together in a descriptive phrase but cringe when the little angel utters an expletive. Where did she get that four-letter word? Most likely from you! She's been listening to and copying your speech for months or years and has probably been rewarded for doing so by your hugs and kisses. So what's up when you get angry and recoil in embarrassment as she blurts out "damn it!" when she knocks over her tower of blocks? Sure doesn't seem fair to her that you reward some utterances but get angry with others!

Knowing that your little one will imitate just about anything that she hears coming out of your mouth should put you on red alert. Be careful what you say, especially in anger, as you just may hear it again from her, and perhaps in public. Breaking yourself of swearing may seem a daunting task, but as with any negative habit, consistent attention to your behavior can curtail offensive words. Remember, it's better to avoid initiating her swearing behavior than to have to stop an existing problem—so try to train yourself to exclude profanity from your own vocabulary before she even picks it up.

But if the kid has already been exposed to bad language and is beginning to use it in an experimental, imitating fashion, the best tactic is to try to ignore it. That includes not showing your surprise or anger, or even laughing at the utterance. All of these reactions are attention-givers, and with most kids, receiving attention for a behavior usually increases its future frequency. So try to ignore the inappropriate language and it will cease if it is not reinforced by yourself, other adults, or siblings (who may think that their little sister's "damn it!" is the cutest thing). Sometimes, though, a short and simple explanation that the swear word is inappropriate may make sense to the 3-year-old and can curtail the issue without too much attention being given to the offensive behavior.

Resolution for grade schoolers: As we've seen, the swearing behavior of preschoolers is usually not intentionally provocative, but the bad language of the grade schooler can definitely be purposeful. These kids may hear offensive words at school, at home, playing with friends in the neighborhood, or at the movies. Nasty language is not difficult to find and many kids think that using it is either cool, attention getting, grown up, an "in your face" maneuver, or just plain funny.

Calling someone a "butthead" seems to be a universal statement on all playgrounds. Kids tend to become obsessed with toileting language as well as body parts and fluids, and most have experimented with using these as descriptors. Calling someone a "snotty face" gets your attention as you visualize what that would really look like. Swearing and bad language are normal kid behaviors, but no matter how typical they are, the utterances can be humiliating and anger-provoking to parents and teachers.

What to do if your grade schooler gets into the habit of uttering swear or potty words? First, put it into perspective—most likely your grade schooler is just trying to be cool or is imitating what the kids are saying. Or if he's in a rebellious stage, the "You're stupid, you can't make me!" or the "hell with it" comment may be directed at getting you angry or involved with him. As with the little kids, it's best to try ignoring the nasty language if it just seems to slip out and he appears to be as shocked as you at the utterance. If that's the case, just redirecting his attention may work. However, if the offensive language

becomes a habit, you should attach a significant negative consequence to it. In this way he'll *better remember* that swearing or inappropriate language is not acceptable and will work on improving his
vocabulary.

However, the child who purposefully swears in order to show
who the boss is or to intimidate parents or peers is a horse of a different color. The basis for this type of offensive language is most
likely a symptom of another problem—perhaps poor self-concept,
feeling left out, believing parents to be unfair, or just not making
it socially with other kids. If this is the case with your child, sit
down and talk it over—try to ascertain why the youngster is so
angry, fearful, or rebellious. Work out a plan of action that rein-
forces good behavior that your child will be proud of, rather than
having to resort to bad language in order to gain attention or shock
value. Your child will appreciate your time and effort to get him
over this emotional hurdle and may not have to resort to bad language in the future.

Resolution for tweens and teens: Kids at this age *know* when
they are using inappropriate language, and do so either out of habit
or to fit in with their cohorts who are also swearing like sailors! If
you find the behavior to be offensive, let the culprit know what ex-
pletives are acceptable in your home, and which ones are not. Many
times during therapy I'll help a family to develop a list of appropriate
words that may be used in the home. Some may be of the four-letter
variety but are deemed to be acceptable by Mom and Dad. Next, we
set up a behavioral system to deal with mistakes made. If anyone (including parents) utters an unacceptable swear word, then the of-
fending party must put money into a "dollar jar." At the end of the
month the family uses this money to go out to dinner, a movie, or
another type of excursion. Even though the family members benefit
from the dollar jar field trip, no one likes having to cough up cash

for every swear word uttered! This is a great way to curtail Dad's slipups and Mom's inappropriate language when frustrated. It teaches kids that their folks will literally put their money where their mouth is and not be hypocritical by cursing themselves but not allowing swearing by the children.

Even if you get the offensive language down to a dull roar in the house, don't expect that your kids will be swear-free with their friends. Many tweens and teens use curse words at school, when out with their friends, or shooting hoops on the courts. It comes with the territory and is a difficult habit to break when surrounded by others who may use more four-letter words than verbs. If you happen to overhear your child swearing in front of her friends, don't be surprised. It may be best to let it go if it is only occasional and a slipup while she's yakking on the telephone. Remember, with teens it's usually best to carefully pick your battles—you don't want to win this one only to lose the war!

The Ultimate Taboo: Getting a Tattoo

Problem: Kids have the amazing habit of wanting to do things their way, even if it goes against the grain of your family code of values. And this seems to be strongest during the teen years. For example, let's say that your 16-year-old daughter is driving you nuts about getting a tattoo—she just absolutely, positively has to have one in order to be happy. To hear the kid talk it's as if she won't be allowed to sit with her buddies at lunch unless she comes to school adorned with a rose petal on her left ankle. Throw into the picture that she's a generally compliant child who makes adequate grades at school, and except for a few forays outside of the boundaries of acceptable behavior, she's usually polite.

You, however, may disapprove of tattoos in general and especially for your kid. Tattoos may bring to mind drunken sailors, women of the night, or gang members, and you'll be darned if your child will be sporting one as long as she's living under your roof. However, your attitude is not playing well with the kid and she becomes insistent, demanding, and moody when the two of you try to discuss it. What to do?

Resolution: First, try to understand why a tattoo has become so important to her. Desiring a tattoo does not necessarily indicate that your child is having emotional or behavioral problems. In fact, the Council of Better Business Bureaus reported a study showing that 1 in 10 adolescents had a tattoo, and over 50 percent of the kids questioned noted that they wished that they could have one. What does a tattoo signify to an adolescent and why is it so alluring?

For many, a tattoo helps them with a sense of identity—it can connote belonging to a select group (perhaps risk-takers, nonconformists, tough kids, or the rose-on-the-ankle crowd). Other teens are attracted to the permanence of a tattoo—the very thing that parents take issue with. Many adolescents see their lives as constantly in flux—parents divorcing, family transitions, uncertainties as to which clique they belong to on a weekly or monthly basis, and romances that end almost before they are begun. Many kids have mentioned to me that, "At least my tattoo will be there—it's permanent and I chose it."

Also, consider the status that a tattoo can bring to a teen. From their point of view, it may be a symbol of power ("I had the guts to endure the pain") or control ("I talked my folks into letting me get one" or "I got tattooed even though my parents forbade me to do so"). Status is important to most of us, but especially to a teen who has to worry about being accepted by peers on a daily basis. Others consider tattoos to be a fashion statement or a work of art. Adorning oneself with a classic design can be seen as enhancing your looks, much the same as a stylish, but perhaps extreme, haircut can be an attention-getting statement.

Now that you understand why your daughter is so adamant about getting a tattoo, it's time for *her* to listen to *your* thoughts. If she has convinced you (and I personally would think that you were nuts) that a small rose petal, perhaps placed in a nonvisible location on her body, is appropriate, then the issues to be dealt with are fairly clear-cut.

1. Select a professional artist who subscribes to the strict health standards of the industry.

2. Agree upon the design of the tattoo and where it will be placed.

3. Decide who will pay for the tattoo.

4. Understand that tattoo removal is expensive, painful, and frequently unsuccessful.

However, if you are still adamantly opposed to the idea even after listening to her argument, be prepared to stick to your guns! As a psychologist I believe that the parent not only has the right but also the responsibility to call the shots, especially when health issues or body modification are concerned. Be clear, concise, and specific with your decision. "You will not be allowed to have a permanent tattoo placed on your body while you are living in this house and I am responsible for you. I feel that at 16 you have no way of knowing how it will impact your life at 20, 30, or 40. The tattoo may cause you great embarrassment when you're in college or looking for a job, and it may also affect how others perceive you. When you are on your own and are an adult, your body will be your responsibility and you'll be able to make these decisions for yourself. At this time the answer is "no" and you must abide by my wishes."

If your child is especially defiant, she may find a way to get a tattoo without your permission. If you think that this is a possibility, warn her ahead of time that you will look into having it removed, and she will be responsible for the cost of the procedure. You may even want to describe how this is done in some appropriately grisly detail. Hopefully she'll realize that it's a battle not worth fighting and leave her tattoo phase to a little later in her life.

Saying "no" to a kid is not fun, but in many cases it's necessary to do so in order to protect her from making a serious, permanent mistake. It takes guts to parent effectively—it's often not easy, but if you listen to your child as well as trust your values and instincts, you probably won't go wrong.

LIVING THE LAW

Understand human development. Accept that *beginnings* (entering preschool, grade school, middle school, and high school) and periods of *intense change* tend to go hand-in-hand with new, sometimes difficult behavior.

Be creative. In dealing with developmental changes, employ a combination of listening/communication skills, keeping an open mind, and being ready to set clear, fair, and firm guidelines.

Don't take it personally. Whether the difficult behavior is biting, swearing, a campaign for body modification, or any other quirky behavior or attitude, it's probably not directed at you. You're neither an awful parent nor is your kid a terrible person. The behavior may be trying, awful, or terrible, but the person is usually okay. Accept this and focus upon behavioral or attitudinal changes.

Realize that problems grow, too. As kids get bigger, often so do their problems. That's part of the child-rearing deal and it comes with the territory. If you are flexible and creative, I know that you can come up with a plan, technique, or consequence that will work—either by compromising with the kid or motivating behavioral change by giving an effective consequence.

Recognize that raising kids can be a good news, bad news process. Try to bask in the new, exciting skills and behaviors, but be ever watchful about the innovative, manipulative techniques that your child comes up with as he matures!

LAW #20

The Law of Bickering:

Squelch Sibling Squabbles

Yes, it's normal for siblings to tease, spar, and taunt each other, but it doesn't mean that they have to do it at your expense. Put a stop to this nonsense immediately by employing my bad points system, as well as teaching your kids how to communicate with civil words, rather than with their fists or verbal barbs.

We've never met, but I can tell you right now that if you have more than one child in your house, those kids will fight with each other. Sibling rivalry (whether emotional, physical, or verbal) is universal and as old as time. And as most parents report, our kids fight over the dumbest stuff—who gets what (front seat in the car, the largest piece of cake, to sleep on the top bunk) or who did what to who (looked at, ignored, made faces at, burped at, punched, kicked, licked).

Seemingly harmless as the rivalry may begin, small issues have a way of driving parents nuts over the months and years. Researchers actually study this stuff and have found that about 70 to 80 percent of families report some level of physical violence during conflicts between siblings. And that's not counting the verbal garbage that kids sling at each other ("You're dumb," "Hey, ugly," "Yo, moron"). Why does this happen so frequently?

Over the years I've counseled many families enduring sibling battles and have seen five main reasons.

1. Differences. Kids find themselves living with a sibling whose personality traits are so different that they consistently annoy and drive each other to distraction.

2. Boredom. There's nothing quite like a good bicker or squabble to break up the monotony of a slow summer day.

3. Habit. Cleaning someone's clock may become second nature if you don't like a behavior—just clobber the other guy and see what happens. Fighting can become the sport of childhood and many kids don't care that it bothers their folks.

4. Acceptance. It's allowed and therefore is encouraged. Mom and Dad either look the other way or are consistently inconsistent in giving out negative consequences for the bickering.

5. Resentment. One kid resents the other's status of even being a family member. This is generally a child who has difficulty sharing attention, parental involvement, or material objects.

If these sound familiar, join the club. Many parents tell me that if they had one behavior to pick that they could change in their children, it would be sibling battles and rivalry. Take Joel, for example. He's the single father of Noah and Adam. Joel came to see me about the kids' constant fighting, bickering, and sibling rivalry. Although Adam is older, larger, and stronger at 11 years of age, 8-year-old Noah has the tongue and wit of a shrew. Even with the age difference, their arguments were fairly evenly matched, with Noah throwing around words and Adam throwing around Noah. Usually the squabbles would end in a draw—Adam's feelings would be hurt and Noah's arms bruised. Well, it really wasn't a draw, as all involved, including Joel, felt badly following a particularly grueling day in the boxing ring. The kids got their verbal and physical licks in, and Joel was left angry, annoyed, and frustrated. It was hard enough raising the kids without the help of their mother (who resided out of state), and he had had it with the senseless bickering.

Joel told me about their typical fights—almost always beginning over a meaningless act, gesture, or word. One kid would look at the other and smile and that could be enough to provoke a battle. Noah had the annoying habit of humming during meals or car rides, and Adam just couldn't stand it. He'd punch Noah, which only resulted in a squeal or a punch in return. Joel would threaten to stop the car and return home, or if the ruckus was during dinner, the meal was ruined.

Joel was also concerned that the boys' sparring meant that they weren't friends and that they might grow up feeling animosity for each other. He confided to me that he often felt incompetent as a parent when his kids began to fight, as if it was his job to make sure that the guys not only didn't kill each other but that they actually enjoyed their relationship. As he spoke, I could feel Joel's pain—as the single most important guiding force in his children's lives he had taken on the responsibility of *making* his children get along as well as respect and enjoy each other.

I informed Joel that his intentions were great, yet unrealistic and logically faulty. No one can *make* anyone like someone else. When it comes to family relationships, it's a matter of *goodness of fit* between personalities. We are born with many of the seeds of our individual temperament. Some kids are naturally easy-going and relaxed. Others tend toward being edgy and hyper, oversensitive and often overreactive to even the slightest stimulation (be it physical or emotional). Then there are the differences between introverts and extroverts, quiet kids versus those who can't seem to refrain from humming, wiggling, and constantly beating out tunes on the air drum no matter how annoying it is to others.

After meeting and talking individually with each of Joel's boys, I could see how they rubbed each other the wrong way. Noah was hyper, sharp-witted, and a real pain in the neck. He seemed to constantly have one body part or another in motion and was talking or making noise incessantly. On the other hand, Adam was a slug. The kid was huge for an 11-year-old and was quite content to hang out on the couch all day, watching TV or playing video games. He told me about his little brother's tendency to disrupt his video viewing by changing the channel without permission, pounding him with pillows, or making disgusting noises.

Noah complained about how his brother would *never* play with him. Although he recognized the difference in their ages, he felt that Adam was a snob and needed to give him more attention. Noah realized that his behavior irritated his brother but felt that it was justified because it provoked some attention from the big lug. He admitted that perhaps he was a bit pesky, but not nearly as severe as Adam portrayed. Noah liked to flick his brother on the arm or to give him a noogie to the head. Adam, of course, perceived these gestures as tormenting, rather than as good-natured teasing.

I described to Joel just how different his children were, and how they were bound to drive each other nuts on a regular basis because of their proximity (living in the same house) and personality trait differences (hyper, humming Noah versus couch potato Adam). And if left undisturbed, their relationship was bound to grow even more disturbing!

Noah, at 8, had many more years of annoying behavior left in him, and Adam was just entering into the tween/teen phase of exceptional moodiness, intolerance, and touchiness. At this point in the conversation, I think that Joel probably would have bolted from town had he not been such a responsible dad. What also helped was my telling him that his kids were not so different from others, but that each was a bit extreme in personality style. And it didn't help that their dad was raising them alone, without the backup and support of a spouse.

At the next session we all met together. First I went to work with the boys. Each was old enough to learn to take responsibility for their behaviors as well as to understand and to respect where the other was coming from. I informed Noah that all of his body parts were under his control and that although he liked to hum, wiggle around, and thump his brother on the head, he had to respect that most people are annoyed by these actions. Noah tried to squirm out of taking responsibility by saying that he couldn't help it, that his hand sort of reflexively flicked Adam's head, or that burps or even more disturbing noises just erupted from his body cavities.

I informed Noah that that was a bunch of baloney—sure these actions were habitual, but he could feel a burp coming on and tone it down, and his fingers did not have a mind of their own. I told him that his job for the next week, until we met together again, was simply to knock it off. He could tone down the fidgeting and thumping if he really wanted to, and I was determined to find a way to motivate his desire to do so. I didn't think that just reasoning with the kid would succeed—Joel had been asking him for years to quit bothering his brother. We needed to enforce consequences for his behavior and Noah was placed on notice that from now on:

• He would receive a bad point from his dad for every purposeful head thump, rude noise, unprovoked pillow fight, or popping of Adam. He would be allowed eight bad points per day (which, trust me, was not a whole lot considering Noah's tendencies). If he kept it to eight or less, he would receive a red $1 allowance poker chip, a blue $1 chip to save to purchase new sneakers, a white privilege poker chip to be saved and traded in for bowling, laser tag, or go-carting, use of electricity, and playtime for the remainder of the day. If his bad point total exceeded eight, Noah would lose all of these rewards that day.

- If his bad points totaled 11 or more, his father was going to give away one of his possessions to the Salvation Army. And Joel was going to rifle through his stuff and make the choice of the soon-to-be lost object—most likely a baseball, video game cartridge, or action figure.

- He was encouraged to ask his father or Adam to play with him rather than to try to tease them into giving him attention. Joel told his son that he would do his best to set aside 15 to 30 minutes each day to play catch or engage in a board game—but only if Noah asked politely and had not exceeded his bad point total for the day.

Next I instructed Adam to:

- Make a list of activities that he would be willing to do with Noah. This took a bit of coaxing, but he finally admitted that playing computer games together would be fun and that he'd give some board games a whirl. Adam made it clear, though, that he didn't want to be teased into playing with Noah—he specifically told him not to come up from behind and pop him on the head, running off hoping that Adam would join in the chase. I encouraged Adam to ignore his brother if he did that and to leave the room. I suggested that Joel make the rule that each boy's bedroom was private and that the other had to have permission to enter. Adam, therefore, would have a refuge to retreat to in order to get a break from his brother's antics.

- Refrain from pounding on Noah. Adam was quite strong and had left marks, brushburns, and bruises on Noah's scrawny frame in the heat of battle, and that needed to cease immediately. We created a new house rule: No physical aggression allowed by anybody. That meant no pushing, shoving, fighting, hitting, or throwing objects. Any aggressive physical action by either boy was to be an automatic loss of a possession to be given to the Salvation Army. Adam would lose, at Joel's discretion, a CD, video tape, game cartridge, or a model airplane. Instead of hitting back, he was to leave the room, calmly tell his father about the incident if he wished, and move on.

• Try to give his little brother some quality time and positive attention. Adam had agreed to try playing computer or board games, as noted above. I explained to him how left out his little brother felt and that some of his annoying manners were probably ploys to gain Adam's attention. Perhaps if Noah felt more accepted by his brother, he wouldn't feel the need to resort to the teasing and taunting.

Finally, I instructed Joel to refrain from asking "Who started it?" when the boys got going. If a verbal squabble began, he was to automatically give each one a bad point. The message to the boys was that bickering would no longer be tolerated. If one started messing around with the other, there was a decision to be made. The victim could:

• Ignore the perpetrator

• Leave the room and go to the sanctity of his bedroom

• Calmly ask his father for help

• Participate in the fight, squabble, tease, or taunt

The first three options would be applauded by their dad, and the last would result in the meting out of bad points for both boys. The bad points would be tallied each day and would result in either receiving or losing rewards. It was each boy's choice, but the message was clear— squabbling would not be tolerated. Bickering is an option—you can engage or disengage, and either choice would result in a consequence. Joel was no longer playing referee—he was now the keeper of the bad points and would give them out in a nonchalant, consistent manner, willing to take away privileges and possessions if necessary.

And the system worked well. I saw the family again the following week, and Joel brought along a log of the kids' bad points. Noah, surprisingly, did slightly better than Adam. All of a sudden this 8-year-old, somewhat-hyper kid seemed to gain self-control of his legs, fingers, and tongue. Although he did push the limits and received six, seven or eight

Sanity Tips for Parents

The following tips can help you keep your cool when your kids are squabbling.

- Realize that siblings often struggle to define how they are different (I'm skinny, you're fat; I'm smart, you're stupid; I'm mature, you're a baby) as well as how they are alike (we're both good athletes, lousy spellers, class clowns). Some of the resentments are based in either being too much alike or too different from each other.

- Don't fret about the kids becoming friends in the future. Remember, it's tough living in the same house with someone who may be annoying or irritating to you.

- Work on motivating your children to develop coping skills that will help them get along with others in the future. Teach them how to listen, to not be defensive, and how to agree to disagree. If more adults had these effective relationship skills, there would be fewer divorces, job changes, and disappointing relationships!

- Understand that older siblings often have the distinct need to be the one in charge or in control. Younger sibs tend to be feisty or annoying, often challenging the authority of the older sister or brother. Some younger siblings feel that they can never measure up to the older one and can easily get their feelings hurt by perceptions of rejection, no matter how unrealistic this is. Keeping this in mind will lower *your* frustration level as you better understand your children's motives.

bad points a day, Noah received his rewards on six of the seven days! Joel kept his word and played catch, rode bikes, and went inline skating with him on the days that he stayed within his bad-point limit. Adam played cards most nights with Noah and hesitantly admitted that it was "almost fun." Although Adam had lost two possessions (a CD and a video tape) to the Salvation Army for smacking his brother, he had otherwise shown considerable restraint by ignoring many of Noah's taunts.

Joel was pleased with the boys' progress but still concerned that they didn't seem close with each other. I allayed some of his fears by telling him that most siblings fight (either verbally or physically) and many are not particularly close during the grade-school years. I implored Joel to focus on the positive—the toning down of the squabbles rather than the few eruptions that had occurred during the week. Also, the kids were beginning to play together more, and that was a good sign. Joel had little control over whether Noah and Adam would end up best buds in the future or not. That was their road to travel over the next several years, and their decision to make.

With maturity comes sensitivity, tolerance, and acceptance of others. As the boys grew I had no doubt that their interests would become more in tune with each other, that Noah would become less hyper and that they would develop greater common ground. Whether they become true friends is out of Joel's hands, but at least he will no longer be allowing them to clobber and annoy each other at will. Noah and Adam would now have a chance to develop a friendship, no longer squabbling because of habit or lack of consequences.

LIVING THE LAW

Teach your kids communication skills. To best help your family with sibling squabbles, try to teach your children to communicate their complaints, gripes, and grumps about each other appropriately. To help avoid miscommunication, consider the following:

- Acknowledge the feelings that the kids are expressing.
- Help them to label feelings accurately.
- Teach them to create compromises or other actions that will resolve the problems.
- Set guidelines for future behavior when the conflict occurs again.

Be prepared to use a bad-point system. If the kids continue to be unreasonable and you see that miscommunication is not the problem, consider using a behavior management program. Include in your system loss of privileges and possessions as well as the ability to earn rewards.

Realize that sibling squabbles are normal. Most kids fight, tease, and even become aggressive with brothers or sisters.

Step in. If you're allowing it, you're encouraging it. Realize that if you let a lot of this nonsense go on, you are actually supporting the battles.

Don't be consistently inconsistent. If you say that you will be giving a negative consequence for bickering, do it and don't back down!

Don't play judge and jury. Try to catch yourself asking the kids "Who started it?" It really doesn't matter, and they probably will blame each other, so what's the point? Just give all of the involved parties a bad point and move on! Of course, you should listen to real concerns and emotional meltdowns, but the daily sibling squabbles are a no-win situation. If you stay out of the way, many kids will either resolve the problem, learn to ignore the sibling annoyance, or decide to take some quiet time in their bedrooms.

Try not to compare the kids. Children are always on the lookout for your "favorite," and even though you love them the same, you probably like different things about each of the kids. Try to compliment when deserved and direct constructive criticism to the action, not the child.

LAW

The Law of the Teen:

Watch, Listen, and Take a Stand

Has your teenager scared the willies out of you lately by going to bed as Dr. Jekyll and waking up as Mr. Hyde? Do you worry that this kid, who you seemed to know fairly well until a year ago, prefers to confide in others and no longer in you? Well, join the club—most parents of teenagers endure these fears. But you can come out at the other end in one piece if you effectively employ these parenting tactics.

have always felt conflicting emotions about teenagers. On the one hand, I envy their youthful spirit, naiveté, and buoyancy, yet on the other, my heart breaks for them. The spontaneity of the adolescent years is uplifting, but the cruel culture that often pervades social groupings in middle and high school scares the wits out of me. Others are noticing, talking, and writing about our teens and how they are faring with peer pressure, fear of social rejection, and the myriad of choices to be made during these years.

Dr. William Pollack in his works *Real Boys* and *Real Boys' Voices* eloquently portrays how playful, expressive young boys evolve into displaying the "Boy Code" at ever earlier stages of development—a tough, almost insensitive appearance molded by the holding in of feelings. Letting it out with a good cry just isn't acceptable, and Dr. Pollack and others hypothesize that this is why so many males become ill, unhappy, or even violent as they mature. Boys, although internally sensitive, learn to put on the appearance of toughness. They often underreact to frustrating, hurtful situations until they no longer can restrain the emotions, and then they may blow—either physically or emotionally.

And then there are the teen girls. Dr. Mary Pipher's *Reviving Ophelia: Saving the Selves of Adolescent Girls* looks at the effects of the state of the family, peer pressure, and lack of values upon teenage girls. Although teen girls do not act out violently with the frequency of boys, they display their own brand of behavior and identity crises, especially as they travel from the preteen through the adolescent years. Whether emoting for them is tolerated, allowed, or encouraged, preschool girls cry much more frequently than do boys. In grade school they whine, complain, and cry more, and by middle and high school they run circles around the guys in terms of crying (once again), spreading rumors, and expressing just about every thought that crosses their minds. In short, girls learn to emote and show and share their frustrations. In the process, though, many parents are held hostage to their whims, moodiness, and teenage tantrums.

Teenagers populate a good 50 percent of my practice. Normally these kids come into counseling with a less-than-thrilled attitude, afraid that therapy will result in some form of punishment, or that they will be misunderstood. Just one more adult taking their parents' point of view. Some, though, especially the angry ones, are glad to have the forum to dump their gripes—they can't wait to unload their feelings of frustration and anger about how unfair Mom or Dad is or how tough it is to fit in socially at school. These kids have little trouble communicating. In fact, sometimes it's difficult for me to get a word in edgewise.

Then there are the depressed teens. Along with sensitivity, introspection, and the exquisite sense of peer radar come the twisted misperceptions of overreaction, oversensitivity, and extreme self-absorption. These misperceptions can mean that almost anything that they say or do outside the home is subject to becoming the center of attention for anyone and everyone. At school a bad hair day can be disastrous—as if the other kids will notice. I attempt to teach teens to just relax and not be so sensitive about everything. The trick is to get a teen to realize that the other kids are involved in so much self-absorption and insecurity of their own, that they rarely think of anyone but themselves. Unfortunately, I have to admit this is usually like talking to a wall, though. So their hypersensitivity and anxiety remain.

This hypersensitivity puts adolescents in a near-constant state of panic, believing that what they say or what they wear will be made fun of and the topic of the lunchroom for the next week. So they search for conformity. But it's not just in dress and speech that they try to conform. They also can't appear too dumb or too smart or it will set them apart from others. So that can mean hiding intellect and ambition, foregoing a skill or gift, going along with a crowd whose behavior is unsafe or doesn't really match their basic values, or withdrawing almost completely from the whole social scene.

Yet some make it through adolescence in one piece, seemingly unscathed. What are these hardy, almost invulnerable kids or their parents doing that allows or encourages this success? According to Judith Rich Harris, author of *The Nature Assumption: Why Children Turn Out the Way They Do*, it's mostly genetics, a pinch of luck, and a spoonful of involved and insightful parenting. Although I agree with Dr. Harris's stress upon genetics as an important aspect in how our kids turn out, I've seen that smart, gutsy parenting goes a long way in terms of keeping our adolescents on track.

Set the Stage for Good Teen Self-Esteem

I've found that there are many things that parents can do that not only help their kids to better survive adolescence but that also help parents to come through this period sane and in one piece. In our efforts to help our teens, we should try to set them on course for developing a good self-concept as well as providing discipline so that their behavior remains within reasonable bounds. In setting the stage for good teen self-esteem and behavior, I've realized you can either stand aside, cross your fingers, and hope for the best, or you can:

- Pick your battles wisely, letting the little stuff go while digging your heels in on the bigger issues.

- Try to understand how the teen feels, perceives, and defines her world.

- Endeavor to remember how being 13 was for you (luckily I've kept an old diary and it confirms many of my not-so-fond memories—mostly of loneliness or feelings of rejection).

- Become informed about today's adolescent culture and is-sues—fear of AIDS, prevalent sexual activity (oral or other-wise), peer pressure, depression, and substance use and abuse.

- Understand your child's quest to be their own persona, within the constraints of tremendous peer pressure to conform to often arbitrary social rules and regulations.

- Learn about lunchroom politics that may be quite cruel.

- Accept that buff (for guys) and thin (for girls) is in, whether it's healthy or not.

- Find and retain the guts to parent wisely, even though your teen may profess to hate you at the moment.

- Understand the lure of substance use and find out what you can do to better drug-proof and alcohol-proof your child.

- Learn to listen *effectively* even though the kid is being unreasonable, bullheaded, or just downright selfish.

- Set rules that are fair, clear, and capable of being followed consistently.

- Figure out how to rescue your kid from the claws of the MTV culture.

- Promote a sense of spirituality that will assure your child a lifetime of direction even though there will be lots of curves in the road.

- Implement the family code of values that necessitates giving to others, not just taking.

- Instill a desire for involvement—be it in sports, hobbies, academics, or volunteering—anything that gets their butts off the couch and stimulates the use of their minds and hearts.

I have a confession to make. Having written several parenting books focusing upon discipline and academic achievement, I've earned somewhat of an "Attila the Hun" reputation—not only in the public but at home with my husband and two kids as well. Even for me, with my Ph.D., counseling practice, several parenting books under my belt, and this stern image, I sometimes find it hard to do what is right for my own kids. I have to admit that my Achilles heel is guilt—just manipulate me into believing that I've hurt your feelings, snubbed you in some way, cheated you, or been unfair, and you'll find that you own me. So even though I'm well trained to out-manipulate the manipulator, the guilt trap has been known to sneak up on me and boy, can I get suckered in.

As an example, let me tell you about my son, Chris. One day when he was 17, Chris was in the computer room instant messaging some friends on the Internet. Picture this: I was minding my own business when he came to me and asked if he could "snow cap" his hair. To the uninitiated in teen hair fashion, this means bleaching just the tips of the hair. As an athlete, Chris had always worn his hair short, never seeming to even notice if it was combed, so his request really came out of left field.

Being the guilt-prone, introspective psychologist-Mom that I am, I couldn't just take this as an impulsive, random request—I had to analyze it closely and from every angle. I wondered whether he was thinking that he would fit in better with the guys if his hair was more in style, or whether he was concerned about his looks or attracting girls as the beginning of the new school year approached. From 0 to 60 in about 15 seconds flat, I had turned his simple request into a search for self, belonging, and meaning. And who am I to overlook such a profound moment in his life?

"Okay," I thought, "lots of my teenage clients have bleached hair (or worse)," and since Chris has always been rather conservative, I opened to the idea. "What the heck, it will grow out quickly if you don't like it, but check with Dad first" was my answer. What transpired next was truly amazing, and I hope that you will keep it in mind when dealing with your own children.

I watched as he rather gingerly approached my husband. "Dad, can I snow cap my hair?" My husband's response was quick, unanalyzed, and to the point: "Chris, don't be an ass. You don't have to do that just because some of the other guys have and they may think that it's cool. You look fine the way you are." Short, simple, honest, and to the point. A real guy type of answer (forgive me, Dr. Pollack), but it worked! Chris just shrugged, said "okay," and began watching a ball-game on TV with his father. Go figure!

Now I don't think that responding to my daughter in this way would have worked so well or even worked at all. She's much too sensitive and would have probably spent the rest of the day analyzing why her father would have called her such a nasty name. In fact, I've known many teen girls in my practice who have reacted to similar parental retorts either violently (slamming a door or knocking over a chair), with verbal abuse ("Who's really the ass here?"), or too literally ("Dad really doesn't respect me. He thinks that I'm a jerk. I wish that I could just disappear!").

I later questioned Chris about how he felt when my husband had called him an "ass" and he looked at me as if I was nuts. "Dad just didn't want me to do something stupid, that's all he meant by it. Why make a big deal out of it?" Sure, my husband could have used more refined language to get his point across, but you know, the kid really got the message! But in my attempt to understand, rationalize, and be sensitive to teen peer pressure, I was missing the point. A 17-year-old boy raised in our home with our values—good student, athlete, employee, and soon-to-be college student—didn't need to go around dyeing his hair or giving in to the social pressure to look odd just to fit in. This was a reminder for me—a warning that I needed to continue to be alert to how important it is for parents to take stands on values and to consistently let our kids know where the limits are.

I offer this rather embarrassing scenario as an example of how parents tend to fall into the trap of overanalyzing just about everything that our kids say or do. The snow-capping request turned out to be an impulsive question—Chris probably wouldn't have done it even if his father had allowed him. But what is important is that my husband's response reassured me how boundaries are so necessary, how much limit setting is needed, and how well it is accepted if you don't dance around it with your children.

Terrible Teen Transformations

Kids can be tough to deal with, and even tougher to raise. And this is especially true of adolescents. They generally enter into this era as human beings—giddy, rambunctious, talkative, and interested in just about everything. And then something happens—it's insidious and you can't quite put your finger on it, as it doesn't happen overnight. But slowly (usually) your best bud, the little boy or girl who loved to be tucked in and tickled may recoil from your touch (especially in public), starts to share her deepest thoughts with her best friend (rather than you), and becomes obsessed with weight, clothing, or popularity. Your son may drop out of soccer or softball, quit the youth group, and declare that the video arcade is his Mecca. As she begins to menstruate, your daughter's moods may take the entire family for a ride as she reaches unheard of highs when the phone rings but barely survives an evening just sitting home with the folks. And so you ask yourself, "What have I done to deserve this?" Well, you either gave birth to or adopted the kid and most likely that's about it.

Most teens face unbelievable pressure on a daily basis—in fact, adolescence is often a culture of cruelty.

Katie, a 14-year-old who was seeing me for depression, related how she would leave for school every morning dressed in a Mom-approved outfit but would change into a skimpy halter top and tight jean shorts as soon as she arrived at school. She felt guilty going against her mother's standards but couldn't face the ridicule that she believed would ensue if her outfit didn't fit the girl fashion code. She really was angry at having to do this, but instead of turning the anger outward, it spread within, leading to the depressive symptoms of appetite suppression and sleeplessness.

Michael dealt with peer pressure in a different way. Sixteen and convinced that whatever he had to say would be either laughed at or ignored, he spent his junior year in high school eating lunch in the library every day. Being prone to denial, Michael would kid himself into thinking that *he* was the one rejecting others and that getting his homework completed in school was more important than hanging with the guys in the cafeteria.

Thirteen-year-old Marcella, after having been dumped by her boyfriend of three months, literally took things into her own hands when she felt that she could no longer tolerate the loneliness and humiliation. She started cutting on her thighs and stomach, places she felt were safe from her parents' inquisitive eyes. Marcella explained, as do so many cutters, that "At least I feel something. It doesn't really hurt. At least I can feel again."

Katie, Michael, and Marcella are not that unusual. Certainly not every adolescent changes clothes just to fit in, or is frightened to eat in the lunchroom for fear of being rejected, or uses self-abuse to fight depression or to gain control over emotions, but many do. Too many. The 9- or 10-year-old who would "tell" on cruel friends now, at 14, may feel that nobody would listen, so he handles it himself (perhaps by holding the feelings inside). The lucky ones may remember and rely on solid advice from their parents or have an astute friend or teacher who intervenes. But many teens do not feel that they have resources to turn to, even if their parents are willing to be involved and, if given the chance, could be very helpful. It's as if the trusting child has turned into a teen who is not sure of herself or her parents' intentions and motives.

I hear about this metamorphosis almost daily in my office—distraught parents wondering where their little kid went and how this odd stranger has returned in his place. It's the opposite of the moth turning into a butterfly, in a behavioral and emotional sense. But it is normal, most teens evolve through this stage intact, and do emerge as that beautiful butterfly again as they enter adulthood. But it's tough as a parent to have the maturity and patience to deal with the adolescent in an effective manner. It takes parental savvy, communication, asking others for help, and continually working with your kid even if she rebuffs you. And most of all it takes guts. You must develop a family code of ethics and values to stand by, not only to serve as a guide for your son, but as a reminder to his parents where the boundaries are (remember Chris and his snow capping? Thank goodness my husband didn't stray from what *we* stood for).

LIVING THE LAW

The adolescent years are a time of extremes—some of your child's greatest memories as well as difficulties will occur between the ages of 13 and 18. This is a time of intense change—physical and emotional, as well as social. So the normal ups and downs experienced by grade schoolers are magnified ten-fold when your kid hits middle and high school.

What's a parent to do? Lots—there are five main areas of parental involvement that can ease your child's transition through this phase and help her to navigate adolescent culture with more success. Let's take a look at these tactics.

Have clear expectations. Teens, even more so than their younger counterparts, need to know what is expected of them—both at school as well as on the homefront. Guidelines, limit setting, and clear, fair rules go a long way in terms of letting your child know how far to push the envelope, what she can get away with, what behaviors are appropriate or inappropriate, and when to go along with the program even if they don't especially want to. Most adolescents are less than thrilled with completing their homework, and they'd much rather watch MTV than plow through their math problems. And that's where you, the parent, come in. If your child knows that there's no TV until homework is completed or the kitchen is cleaned, she'll comply, especially if there is a consequence attached to the requested behavior. Allowances, privileges, bedtime, and electricity (using anything that plugs into the wall or needs batteries with the exception of lights, blow dryers, and alarm clocks) are excellent consequences that will definitely motivate your kid to get moving. Also, limits and guidelines make a child feel secure—they know what is expected of them each day and understand what positive things will occur if they respond appropriately, and what negative consequences will happen if they choose not to comply. Security and permanence are especially important to your kid during the teen years, as just about everything else seems to be in a state of flux.

Keep your adolescent involved in activities. A bored teen is often an unhappy teen. Kids this age thrive on activity—both mental and physical. Those who sit around tend to watch too much TV, eat too much, perhaps spend too much time on suspect Internet chat lines, and often become depressed. Teens are *still children*, and some of the main jobs of childhood are to learn how to be cooperative with others, to have fun, to expend energy and to just goof off. Sadly, though, many adolescents feel the social pressure to resist play, even though in their hearts that is what they yearn for. Playing catch and flag football are not only fun but relieve stress after a long day at school. Play is the stuff of childhood, yet teens often succumb to their friends' notions that anything less than living on the phone or shopping at the mall is politically incorrect. If this is your child, encourage her to get to know the neighborhood kids again and to dust off the bike or inline skates and engage in some real activity. If possible, sign your kid up for a sport team where he'll learn new skills, make friends, increase his self-concept based on his athletic accomplishments, and expend energy in an acceptable fashion. Involved kids are often too busy to get into trouble, to fool around with cigarettes or drugs, or to become depressed. Also, check out the youth group at your place of worship, the school's chess club or debate team, or local theater groups.

Your child will be busier, happier, and more involved, and even though getting your kid to these activities may run you a bit ragged, it sure beats childhood depression or substance abuse!

Teach your teen compassion. Some of the most important needs of children this age are to feel significant, valued, and important. The lucky ones may get these needs met if they are popular with peers, know how to successfully work a crowd, or are the teacher's pet. Most other teens, though, need to work at being significant, and a sure bet is to involve them in an activity that helps others. There's no better way to feel important or needed than to help someone less fortunate than you. Volunteering at a local soup kitchen, daycare center, nursing home or animal shelter helps your child to value the positive things in her own life and will help her to develop a compassion for others not so fortunate. I've noticed time and again that kids who volunteer and help others are much less likely to tease, bully, or harass others. Compassion is not innate—it is learned through experience with a variety of life situations. It's also not a bad idea if you're involved in the activity—leading by example works well and you'll probably feel better for the volunteer time spent with your child.

Encourage dialogue and communication. Whether your teen admits it or not, you are the most important person in his life. Although he may respond with grunts rather than with words, your kid is depending upon you to be there for him—not only to give him a ride to the ballfield or to the movies but also to talk to and listen to his concerns. This does not mean that he necessarily wants your advice or will use it; he may just desire your listening ear. If he needs your suggestions, he'll let you know, especially if you've proven yourself to be a good listener, nonjudgmental, and capable of not interrupting him! One of the biggest gripes that I hear from adolescents is that their folks are so anxious to fix the problem that they just don't take the time to let the kid fully explain the situation—Mom or Dad have already interrupted and Junior shuts down, waiting for the same ol' lecture. If this sounds familiar, try to break the pattern by going for nightly walks when your child can talk if he wants to or the two of you can just be together. Some of the best communicating I've done with my kids has been of the silent variety—just spending time together walking the dog or taking a leisurely bike ride. Being your teen's confidant is not only a responsibility but an honor not to be taken lightly. Also, consider the alternative—if he can't share his concerns with you and depends solely upon his peers for advice, that can be really scary!

Allow and encourage reasonable independence. By adolescence, kids are ready to make many of their own decisions, with and without your guidance. Choices regarding clothing style, friends, study schedule (as long as there is one!), music, and how leisure time is spent are areas that should be within your child's discretion, at least initially. If your son displays good judgment in terms of friend selection, that's great—but if not, you may need to discuss just what it is about his buds that gives you the creeps. If your daughter's clothing choices stay within the school dress code guidelines and you're not too embarrassed to be seen in public with her, then let her call the shots. If it gets too weird, you may need to step in and set up some family guidelines, especially in terms of clothing she is allowed to wear when she's with you or other family members.

Music selection is another dicey area, often leading to conflicts between parents and adolescents. I've witnessed kids who can listen to the nastiest stuff and it doesn't affect their personality or morals. I've also seen teens of the more gullible variety who literally *become* the music that they listen to. These chameleon kids are usually searching for an identity and can easily slip into the persona of the group, whether that's rock, punk, or Gothic. If this is your child, it would be safer to pick another area in which to allow and encourage independence, while keeping tabs on concerts attended and CDs purchased.

It's appropriate, and healthy, to give your kids the control to make certain choices as they mature. Wise selections lead to good self-esteem as kids realize, "I can call the shots and not only am I happy with my selection of friends, but Mom and Dad respect my decisions." Inappropriate choices are actually teachable moments—the child learns firsthand that hanging out with sketchy kids can lead to restrictions or legal problems and perhaps in the future special thought should be given to who is included in his close circle of friends. Some teens have to learn the hard way about independence and decision-making, but often these are the most effective and long-lasting of lessons learned.

Try the above tips and let him be a kid again. They'll help you and your teen make it through one of the toughest phases of childhood. Give your kid permission to be a child again and to engage in activities that are just pure fun and not a mimicry of the teens she sees on TV, at school, or on magazine covers.

The Law of Learning:

Stand Up
for School

You may be surprised at the real reasons behind your kid's whines of "I don't want to go to school." Children can be miserable in school because of social, learning, or anxiety issues—and these don't just go away. Once you understand what's really going on, you can help him overcome these obstacles to education.

Okay—it's Monday morning and you're just getting started. Let's see . . . take the dog out, grab a shower, and wake up the kids to get ready for school. All goes as planned until your 9-year-old son hits you up with, "I don't wanna go to school" and rolls over on his top bunk. Now what? Most likely you've had to deal with this before, and you know that a combination of tickling and firm persuasion usually gets your kid up and moving.

Lots of children don't want to get up and go to school, especially after having a weekend of fun. Hanging around the house and playing with friends sure beats having to pay attention in the classroom—so it's not unusual for children to check to see if you'll cave in and let them play hooky. It's normal if your child tries this out occasionally, as long as he makes it to school without too much fuss. However, it's a whole different ball game if the kid habitually balks at going to school or seems genuinely fearful or anxious about it. Kids, especially in the grade-school years, display school refusal behaviors for three main reasons.

1. They feel at risk socially—rejected, ostracized, or ignored by peers. The school environment may be perceived as lonely, uncomfortable, or threatening. It's tough when you're 7 years old and you feel unaccepted and different from the other kids.

2. Those who perceive themselves as academically inferior often feel picked on or teased by other children when they make errors in class, and many consider themselves to be dumb or stupid because of the teasing. (It's humiliating to answer incorrectly in class with 20 kids watching your unsatisfactory performance.)

3. Children who are very active, perhaps even hyperactive, can become extremely uncomfortable when expected to sit for several hours in the classroom, even with breaks for recess, lunch, and PE. These kids seem to be constantly chastised by their teachers to stay in their seats, to focus on their work, or to keep their hands to themselves.

Children who display one or more of the above problems tend to have school refusal issues at some point in their academic careers. Feeling lonely, dumb, or unfocused would be uncomfortable for just about anyone. Consider the adult who feels rejected by her co-workers at the office—it's no fun thinking that others are talking negatively about you or that they have little to say to you. Or, if you're having trouble completing a project and day after day your on-the-job frustration mounts, leaving work at five o'clock becomes a relief. Or ever feel antsy or edgy because you're cooped up behind a desk pushing papers or answering phone calls, while you yearn to be working outdoors?

Well, just as an adult who feels socially unaccepted, inferior to the task, or incompatible with the work environment would begin to be uncomfortable or unhappy with his job, so do kids with similar problems. It's human nature to avoid an unpleasant situation by calling in sick to work or, for a child, by refusing to go to school. The child with school refusal issues is generally trying to avoid the unpleasantness he perceives waiting for him. So what can you do if this is your kid?

Understand the Reason

First, listen to your child and take her seriously. If there's a pattern of complaints about others not liking her, check it out further. Also, ask the teacher about children your child seems to get along with. Does she have a special friend to sit with at lunch or is she alone? Does she hang around kids at recess? If not, your daughter is legitimately feeling lonely and sad. What can you do? In the grade-school years, it's still possible to help create and cement social relationships for your children. Encourage the teacher to pair her with another child whom your kid would like to get to know better. You can also jumpstart friendships by inviting classmates home to play after school or on weekends. Get to know the other moms and dads—some are probably in the same boat, looking to help their kids establish relationships with their classmates.

Also, check out organizations such as Cub Scouts and Brownies, sports teams, or chorus and band—kids with similar interests tend to get along well, and their mutual experience helps conversations flow easier.

If your child fits into the second category leading to school refusal—that of being weak in an academic area or two—assessment and remediation should do the trick. Consult with your child's teacher or guidance counselor to get information on achievement testing. After you understand the nature and causes of the weak areas, check into tutorial situations, both at school as well as privately. If your child's testing meets certain criteria, he should be eligible for special programs providing individualized instruction to bring his knowledge, grades, and skills up to par. The process may be lengthy, so try to get started as soon as you notice a deficit area developing.

Once your child feels more comfortable with the work, he'll feel smarter and more confident. The I-hate-school problem will tone down as he begins to look forward to answering questions in class and is no longer nervous about participating in front of his peers.

The third group of kids, those antsy, fidgety Phils, present a challenge for even the most seasoned teachers. It's difficult to remain diplomatic when a kid is constantly getting out of his seat, wiggling around, dropping pencils, or talking to his neighbor. Teachers often resort to reminding, nagging, and disciplining fidgety, overactive kids much more than their quiet, self-controlled counterparts. Often this makes children feel singled out and picked on by the teacher, leading to anxiety about coming to class the next day.

There are three ways to keep your antsy, unfocused child on task: use a reward system for completing work in the classroom, provide academic remediation for knowledge gaps in weak areas, and consider medication for kids who are diagnosed with Attention Deficit Disorder. These techniques generally help children to focus on their work rather than on the contents of their neighbor's pencil box, as well as helping them to keep their bodies in their seats.

It's amazing what a reward system will accomplish if the consequences for completing class work, staying in the seat, and not making car noises during math class are important and consistently delivered! Once your child realizes self-control and success via one or more of these methods, he'll feel on top of the work in the classroom and less worried about being "picked on" by the teacher or others.

What to Expect as Your Child Moves to Middle and High School

School refusal generally decreases dramatically as children grow older. Although social rejection still can play a major role in adolescence, the sheer size of most middle and high schools lends itself to kids finding a buddy or two. Also, many academic problems have been worked out by then—either through direct remediation, compensation, or inclusion in a special program at school. In addition, the fidgety second grader usually becomes calmer by middle school and no longer is constantly chided by teachers to sit still. He may still be displaying inattention, but generally this does not lead to behavior-based referrals or classroom embarrassment.

There is a light at the end of the tunnel—the Monday morning chorus of, "I hate school, do I hafta go?" decreases as your child gets older. The trick is to decipher what's motivating the school refusal behavior and to take the appropriate steps toward remediation.

LIVING THE LAW

Worried about your child's school performance, attitude, or academic self-confidence? Check out the following suggestions.

Have a heart-to-heart chat with your kid. Is he refusing to go to school because he feels socially outcast or academically inferior, or could it be that he's uncomfortable because he just can't sit still? Often your child will know and can talk about what is really going on at school, especially if you've already worked on Law #16, The Law of Communications.

If your child is clueless, check with the teacher. Often a savvy teacher has a hunch about what's really cooking with your kid. But, if she's unsure as to the basis of the problems, it may be wise to seek professional help for specific recommendations.

Contact your school counselor to set up a complete psychoeducational evaluation. This will help to determine your child's strengths and weaknesses in order to begin a program of remediation. It may be beneficial to set him up in a special class or program to meet his unique needs, or after-school tutoring or remediation just may do the trick.

Set up a study skills program. If you see that your child is disorganized in school or during homework time and the psychoeducational evaluation shows no deficits, then it's a matter of teaching him good study skills. Use a daily assignment sheet that the child fills in and each teacher signs to validate that the homework and test dates are accurate. The child uses this guide to determine what books and folders need to be taken home each day. Next, make sure that homework is completed in a timely fashion. Quiz the kid to make sure that he's comprehending what he's reading, and review what he doesn't seem to know. Teach him to pack his organizer and book bag at night, so that in the morning he's ready to go. You may find that Law #6, The Law of Structure, is beneficial in motivating your child to learn and employ good study skills.

If your child is socially anxious, let him know that he's not alone. Many children go through a period of feeling alone, invisible, or "out-of-it." Help to begin or cement new friendships by contacting some classmates' parents to set up playdates. All your child may need is one good friend to sit with at lunch or to play with at recess to feel on top of the world. She'll gain confidence and social skills as her relationships progress. It's not only okay, but at times necessary, for parents to jumpstart friendships and to promote pro-social behavior in their children.

LAW #23

The Law of
Patient Parenting:

Keep Your Cool

Don't kid yourself, you can't do everything. The more you try to cram into your kid's day, the more stress and strain it puts on your family life. Don't forget, having a family is supposed to be fun! Prioritize, delegate, breathe deeply, and smile. Your patience and attention are some of the most valuable gifts you can give your child.

ace it, you're only human. Sure, you had this vision of doing it all—working in a career, raising kids, and even fitting in some fun time with your spouse or just by yourself. Then reality hits and you've realized that this multitasking stuff just isn't what it was cracked up to be. Far from feeling like we have it all, this Jack-of-all-trades-master-of-none approach leaves most parents feeling like we never quite seem to have enough of anything. And at the same time, we have too much—too many responsibilities, too many things to do, too many things we have to learn with too little time to deal with them. This stress triggers anxiety, edginess, and a lack of tolerance and patience with family members—especially with the kids.

This reminds me of one of my favorite clients, Diane. Check this out—she's a single mom of three very rambunctious girls. She receives, in her opinion, insufficient child support and therefore works two jobs. After dropping her angels off at grade school, she rushes to meet her first client at the hair salon. Not only does she do hair, but she also listens to problems all day long and has to be nice about it! Believe me, I know that's no picnic! (But at least I don't have to cut bangs during my sessions.) At 3:30 P.M. she's back at the kids' school in the car pickup line, taking the girls to their grandmother's for after-school care. Grandma fixes them all a very early dinner (thank goodness), and Diane at least gets to eat with the kids. Then it's off to the gym where she teaches aerobics classes until 7:30 P.M. Back in the car, pick up the kids (again, thank goodness that Grandma has supervised their homework), and on to the bedtime ritual.

One of the girls is in charge of nuking the popcorn, while the others put away the day's stuff and tidy up the house. Diane takes a shower, and they watch a half-hour of television or play a board game while chomping down their snack. Then it's time for baths, teeth brushing, and a snuggle as each girl is tucked into bed. Then Diane gets to hit the sack. Not a lot of fun, but this woman is trying hard to keep it all together and the family is getting by.

It wasn't always this tight, though. When she was married to Rich, she worked 3 days a week as a hair stylist and was able to pick up the girls from school and fix dinner most nights. The older two were in ballet, and there was always time to visit Grandma or go to the park so that the girls could run off some steam. Since their separation and divorce 2 years ago, Diane has adapted to her hectic schedule and does her best to keep the family on track. But she is running out of patience. She recently noted to me that she gets snippy with her mother—even though without her help she'd be up a creek—and intolerant of her clients' whining and complaining about the inconveniences in their lives. If they only knew what Diane was going through!

And then there are the girls. Even the best-behaved children can come across as demanding or whiney at times, and this mom has just about had it. Being responsible not only for herself but for the well-being of three little ones can be overwhelming, especially when finances are tight and time is limited. I told her that it wouldn't be unusual for *anyone* in her situation and with her tight schedule to be short-tempered and snippy with their children. In fact, she's behaved rather admirably under the circumstances. She needed to give herself a break and to accept that at this point in her life, at least, things will not be as calm, easy, or comfortable as she'd like for her family. It's tough to accept that, but once you do, you can relax a bit and quit piling on the guilt!

Now I realize that Diane's situation is somewhat extreme, but keeping your cool as a parent can be tough for just about anyone. And the stress is often exacerbated if you're edgy about your job, short on time, have kids with lots of extracurricular activities, or your children are especially noncompliant. *No one*, and let me repeat that, *no one* can keep their patience all of the time. It's an emotional impossibility so don't even try to go there! What is realistic, though, is to strive to make some changes that will allow you to become a more patient parent, and the entire family will reap the rewards.

Patience is truly a gift, as well as a skill to be developed. As with acquiring any other talent, it takes practice, compromise, and actually setting a goal. Try baby steps first, such as counting to 10 before raising your voice, and then moving on to higher-level skills such as developing a different perspective or changing your parenting and family priorities. I'm sure that there will be setbacks, but the more you keep your cool with your children, the less stress there will be in your household or carpool. And your kids will take notice and just might begin to model a more tolerant attitude themselves!

LIVING THE LAW

Keep your expectations realistic. Remember that there are only 24 hours in a day, and some of that must be devoted to work (at the office or at home), transportation, mealtimes, sleep, extracurricular activities, checking homework, and organizing for the next day. Trying to stuff 28 hours of activity into 24 never works well, and the entire day may feel incomplete and upsetting. It's psychologically healthier to set limits, guidelines, and structure on your day *up front* rather than to fall behind and feel like a failure at the end of the day. This may mean saying "no" to some of your kids', neighbors', or friends' requests. Sure, they may be a bit disappointed, but keeping your schedule on track will ultimately please you and others much more than gratifying their immediate and perhaps unimportant requests. You may also have to give up some responsibilities in order to keep a realistic schedule. Perhaps you shouldn't be homeroom mom this year, or karate may have to be put on hold in exchange for the family having some dinners together during the week.

Prioritize what really matters to you. Trust me, you can't have it all. With that in mind, put some thought into what's really important to you as a parent. Some families value playing together, others focus upon family meetings or meals together, and still others prefer to be on the go and to catch up with each other only on weekends. Does some downtime sound enticing—paying a babysitter or a neighbor to watch the kids while you and your partner relax, take a nap together, or go out to dinner? When considering what's really important to the family, don't forget to include things that are important to you as an individual. If you're not getting *some* of your own needs met, most likely you'll be out of sorts, short-tempered, and less than patient with the children.

Prioritize what really matters to the kids. I've come to the conclusion that many of the activities that we get so stressed about are self-imposed and unnecessary. Overbooking children is usually a blend of the kids expressing some interest in taking a lesson or joining a club combined with the parent's desire to expose the children to everything and anything. I'm as guilty as the next parent in this regard, and I must confess that by the time my daughter was 11 years old, she had engaged in 17, count them—17, types of lessons or clubs. We trudged to the barn for horseback riding, the courts for tennis, the pool for swimming, and the gym for tumbling. Then there were those awful years taking piano and violin lessons mixed in with ballet and jazz. She was a Brownie and a Girl Scout, a member of a softball league for several years, and a basketball and soccer player. And the list goes on. But the strange part is that of all of the activities, groups, and lessons that the kid was exposed to, she really loved only one thing—and that was softball. Not only was she quite talented, but my husband was her coach and biggest fan for 7 years in a row. Now that was quality time for the two of them, and probably the only one of the many activities that made a positive, significant impact on her life. I shudder to think about the time and money that could have been better spent had she been more assertive about her priorities and I more observant about her talents and desires.

The best way to avoid this trap, I finally learned, is to communicate to your kids that they need to keep you informed as to whether they feel that they are getting anything out of the activities, or are engaging in them out of habit or a feeling of responsibility. Sure, we all want to get our money's worth for lessons that are prepaid, but at times it may make more sense to call it quits and take the extra time for family fun or just plain downtime. Preventing overbooking is obviously prudent, so setting a limit on the number of afternoons or evenings out per week may be a fair and democratic way of deciding how many activities will be engaged in.

Delegate chores. Despite being outstanding students, talented artists, and remarkable athletes, somehow our kids have convinced us that they are either incapable of helping out with household responsibilities or that it would take too much effort to teach them how to proceed with the task. Folks, please listen up here. They *know* how to sweep a floor, make a bed, do the laundry, and feed the dog. They are not dumb—in fact they are very, very smart and cagey! By appearing helpless, children are often allowed to avoid responsibilities. Turns out this trick is being played out in most of my client's households. But not for long. Pull the plug and set up a chore chart that is age-appropriate. Be sure to keep it realistic to your children's developmental stages, set definite time limits by which the chores must be completed, and attach significant consequences (both positive and negative) to task completions. You are not a demanding parent if you insist upon your kids helping out around the home—in fact, you're preparing them for life as an adult, and their future spouses and bosses will thank you for the work ethic that you're establishing early in their lives!

Stop nagging, lecturing, and yakking. You really don't need to repeat yourself when you've made a request—she probably heard you the first time, and definitely by the second! If you attach a consequence that has "teeth" to it (daily allowance, use of electricity—TV, CD player, computer access), she'll probably get it done on time. All that reminding, lecturing, and yakking just annoys and irritates the kid— let your actions speak louder and longer than your words.

Stick to a routine as much as possible. Mornings and evenings seem to be the two most stressful parts of the day. Set up strict getting-ready-for-school schedules as well as bedtime rules (in bed by 8:30 P.M., read a book, lights out by 9:00 P.M.). And there's no point to setting up schedules if you don't stick to them—expect the routine to be followed and your kids will be more compliant.

Don't take it personally. All children have difficulty at times behaving in restaurants, malls, and in the car. Your child is not acting up to make you angry or to ruin your candidacy for Parent-of-the-Year. He's whining or fussing because he wants what he wants when he wants it—pure and simple. He's dawdling with his homework because it's boring—not to get you mad or to prove that your attempts at teaching study skills are worthless. Child-rearing is not a sprint; it's more of a marathon. Responsible, polite behavior can take years to develop, and there will be many embarrassments along the way. Try to keep this in mind when you're feeling self-conscious about your child's public behavior. Provide a consequence for inappropriate behavior and move on.

When you feel yourself about to blow, have a backup plan. Kids can really push our buttons, and we all need some quick calm-down tricks at our disposal. If your child is fussing in the timeout room, you don't have to subject yourself to listening. As long as he's safe, put on some music that will distract and calm you down. Or how about putting *yourself* in timeout? Have an older sibling watch the fussy little one and sit in the tub or take a relaxing shower. "Taking five" allows you to calm down and think about what you really want to say to your child.

Remember, you can always reprimand later, but you can't take back inappropriate statements made in anger. Saying, "Your behavior is too much. I need some time to think about what I'm going to do. I'll get back with you in 10 minutes," not only gives you the time and space to think clearly, but also allows the child to wonder what fate will befall her! It's a handy trick, one that I've used on many occasions with my own kids as well as suggested to my clients. Finally, consider putting exercise into your daily routine. This doesn't have to mean 45 minutes per day with a personal trainer—a quick walk or jog around the block, doing some crunches or situps, or a workout at the gym can help you blow off steam and keep things in perspective.

Remember, this too shall pass. When you find yourself at wits end, consider whether the current problem will matter tomorrow, next week, or next month. If it won't, let it go. We can't solve all of our kids' problems nor provide for all of their needs. Be realistic and practical, and most of all, realize that at times just getting through the day in one piece is a success. Take the pressure off yourself. You don't need to raise a junior Einstein or a concert pianist to feel like a successful parent. Acquire some patience with your kids' antics and noncompliant behaviors, and you may find your family more fun and your home atmosphere more pleasant.

LAW

The Law of Nonviolence:

Banish the Bullies

Who are the bullies? Who are the victims? And what can you do if you have one, or both, living under your roof? Plenty—from teaching bully-coping skills to encouraging social competence in your own kids. This is one area where children really can't do it alone. They need your help and involvement to keep them safe, happy, and with positive memories of childhood.

Let me tell you about Stephen. This 11-year-old sixth grader was polite, a good communicator, and a really nice kid. He was sensitive and wouldn't hurt a fly. But apparently that can be a problem, especially when you're a slightly built, nonathletic sixth-grade boy. Although most of the girls befriended Stephen, the guys in his class really stuck it to him. He told me that a typical school day might include being called a fag, perhaps getting his pants shanked (pulled down a few inches, usually from behind), and either eating alone or with some girls at the cafeteria table. Life did not feel good for this young man, and it really wasn't his fault. Stephen was becoming more depressed as the school year wore on, and his folks brought him for therapy to see if I could help.

Although kids of all ages can be bullied or be bullies themselves, it tends to escalate in the middle-school years. Children often pick on each other verbally or shove and push a weak classmate. Overweight kids are easy targets, as are children who dress, speak, or act differently than others. It's a shame that our culture allows and perhaps even encourages these types of behaviors, but it's still a reality in many of our school grounds, classrooms, and neighborhoods.

As I worked with Stephen, we discussed his feelings and reactions to the teasing and bullying that he received. We also reviewed what he had tried to do to discourage it—what seemed to work and what had been a dismal failure. According to Stephen, he had *tried everything and nothing had worked*. He said that he had ignored the taunts, but the bullies kept coming. When teased about his poor basketball dribbling, he tried making a joke out of it, bouncing the ball even more haphazardly. This only led to more hoots and hollers from the guys, and he wished that he could just disappear. Stephen's mom had invited the kids over for his 11th birthday party but only two boys showed up along with a bunch of the girls. Stephen, though, said that he had a great time at his party since the kids who did come were truly his friends.

With that realization, Stephen really started himself on the road to a happier life. Once a child realizes what *true friends* are, that's half the battle won. As we worked together, I told Stephen that trying to make his way into the popular guy crowd would probably be a battle and was unrealistic. Anyway, who would want to hang around with those guys? Well, Stephen and just about any kid his age would, as children are usually quite taken with popularity and peer pressure. As adults we understand the ephemeral nature of being cool but kids still don't get it. And many who are obsessed with fitting in don't seem to notice that other kids are in the same situation. Eventually I was able to convince Stephen that he was not alone—that there were other children who felt left out and bullied, but they just didn't advertise it.

I started my campaign to move Stephen into what I like to call the *middle group*—a few children who were like him in terms of sensibilities, interests, and social standing. His particular group grew to contain the two boys, Mark and Frank, who came to his birthday party, as well as Sarah, Katie, and Jana who sat with him at lunch. Stephen's parents did their best to have the boys sleep over whenever possible and to become friends with the other parents. As there is usually safety in numbers, when it became known that Stephen had a group of kids who would stand behind him, the bullying toned down. Why? He now had Mark and Frank as backup and a group of five to sit with at lunch. Sure, it wasn't the most popular crowd and the cool guys didn't go out of their way to be friendly, but they also didn't go out of their way to beat on the kid anymore.

Most of us, like Stephen, have some not-so-fond memories of having been bullied as kids, or of even being the bully ourselves. Looking back as adults it may not make sense to have hurt others or, as victims, to have tolerated the wrath of a bully. But things look different when you're a kid—maneuvering for social position, vying for admiration or attention, and fitting in with the popular crowd may be all that seems to matter during the school years.

As parents we want to help our children to avoid this seemingly senseless situation, or to at least facilitate their understanding as to why kids pick on others. To help get a grip on this, let's consider the latest research on bullies and their victims, and what the best parental interventions are.

Bullies

Bullies are those who use negative actions (generally physical or verbal aggression) against others. Most research has focused upon boys rather than girls. The little we know about female bullying is that girl bullies tend to use tactics different than their male counterparts. Girls often employ *indirect bullying* such as socially isolating their victims by excluding them from the group, teasing, or spreading rumors. Boys tend to use more direct tactics such as hitting, shoving, fighting, or aggressive verbal abuse.

Boy bullies tend to be stronger, larger, and more aggressive than their peers. Some research suggests that bullies are also perceived as athletic, handsome, outgoing, and socially magnetic. Therefore, the movie stereotype of the bully as a defiant social outcast may be more myth than reality. Indeed, bullies tend to hang around other aggressive kids, and make up about 10 to 15 percent of the school-aged population.

When interviewed, grade-school bullies rate themselves as leaders, but the group they lead tends to be aggressive and cliquish, made up of those usually not accepted by more model students. They count on intimidation to raise and keep their status within the peer group. Even though bullies may be seen as hurtful to their victims, their intimidation often provides a certain social status. Other aggressive kids hang around them for protection and affiliation, and bullies are often rated as some of the most popular and socially connected children, especially in the elementary school years. The myth of the "low self-esteem bully" may be just that—a myth, since aggression, especially in males, often equates with status and popularity.

Therefore, bullies, especially those who assume leadership roles, may be those who use aggression *effectively*. There's a great deal of competition for social resources during the school day (attention, friends, and allies), and effective bullies seem to be those who have learned to use their aggression to maintain their leadership role in the peer group.

Victims

Now let's take a look at who these guys are shoving around. Habitual victims (those who seem to be constantly picked on) make up about 18 percent of the school-aged population. Many of us have been pushed around or verbally berated by another kid while growing up, but today, nearly one in five kids seem to be victimized year after year. Victims tend to be smaller, weaker, and shier than their peers. Kids with handicaps (physical, verbal, or learning), children who look different (are overweight, have unique physical characteristics, or who even are just consistently out of fashion) are picked on significantly more often than those who don't stand out.

Victims, especially those who endure teasing or taunts over an extended period of time, tend to develop low self-esteem as well as depression. Statistically, victims are the least attractive, socially inappropriate kids and generally are not aggressive in return. However, *impulsive victims* can overreact, feeding the bully's behavior by giving him just what he wants—attention. This can be seen by the bully as further provocation and may actually heighten the taunts and teasing, especially if the victim reacts in a highly emotional manner.

What You Can Do

As a parent you can definitely tone down bullying at home by setting up clear rules about verbal and physical aggression, and the negative consequences that the kids will receive if they step over the line. This is one area of child behavior where it is absolutely imperative for folks to lay down the law. Bullying and tormenting siblings, friends, or animals should *never* be tolerated in your home, and it's up to you to put a stop to it as soon as you see the perpetrator starting to tease or torment.

It also follows that neither parent should accept being bullied by any of the kids. That may sound ridiculous (or at least it should!), yet I know many moms and more than a few dads who are very reluctant and even actually afraid of saying "no" to their kids or standing up to them. Not only is that intolerable, but it sure isn't doing the kids any good to grow up believing that they can manipulate, torment, or bully adults or peers and get away with it. Yes, it may work in the short run, but the real world will not tolerate that type of behavior, and your child will pay dearly.

LIVING THE LAW

Don't allow physical aggression in your home. Bullies tend to come from homes where physical aggression is used by parents to punish their children, folks have a negative attitude toward their kids, or they tolerate aggressive behavior between members of the family. So try using negative consequences that are not aggressive or physical in nature (such as timeouts or losses of privileges), set limits on how much physical or verbal roughhousing you'll let the kids engage in (if any), and adopt a supportive, positive attitude toward your children.

Teach bully-coping skills. Encourage your child when confronted by teasing or bullying to throw the aggressor off track by making a funny comment. For example, tell your daughter that if the perpetrator continues to tease her about her braces, to respond with something like "Oh, so *you're* the new braces monitor. I didn't realize that!" Or have your son *manipulate* the bully when being teased about his failed attempts at shooting hoops by saying, "Thanks for noticing. I appreciate your interest!" The point is that your child needs to learn to maintain his self-control in these uncomfortable situations and by doing so actually controls the bully-victim relationship. You should role play various responses with your kids until they get good at it. The process can actually be fun!

Encourage social competence. Some victimized children may have deficits in social cognition or social competence. To avoid this, engage your child at an early age in playgroups or playdates, and consider preschool activities as well. As your child matures, continue to encourage group activities so that she learns how to enter into a new group of friends and to effectively work a crowd. Some kids need a boost in terms of learning socially appropriate behaviors, how to read and understand group actions, and starting conversations even in awkward moments. Inclusion in group situations can go a long way in helping your child to feel more comfortable with others.

Help your child to fit in. Children who are socially aware tend not to be picked on as much by others. Sure, this is superficial and it shouldn't be that way, but until we succeed at changing how kids view popularity and they become more humane with each other, I recommend that you expose your children to what's important to kids their age—be it sports, music, movies, or fashion. However, if it looks like your kid is not interested in typical gender- or age-related activities, help him seek out other avenues of interest. Odds are that he'll find a buddy on his baseball team or he'll make a friend through Cub Scouts. You can help initiate and cement friendships by talking with the teacher and finding out which classmates may be good matches for your child. Pursue this by contacting their parents and offering a playdate or a sleepover. Often, kids just need a jumpstart to a relationship and then it takes on a life of its own.

Be assertive about bullying at school. If your kid is being bullied at school, contact the administration about the problem. When students do not tolerate bullying (kids report aggressive behavior to school authorities, interrupt bullying behavior, or defend victims), the rates of victimization and bullying decline. It's possible that the school administration has been giving "implicit tolerance" to bullying on the belief that students must learn to deal with bullies themselves, or that coping with victimization is a normal part of growing up. It doesn't have to be, though. It's becoming apparent that when teachers, school administrators, and the students themselves do not tolerate bullying behavior, the incidence of this abuse decreases significantly. So don't be afraid to talk to school personnel about the issue—it could save your child a lot of grief and misery!

Put it all together. Kids who have buddies, know how to be a good friend themselves, are compassionate with others, and are taught not to tolerate teasing and bullying tend not to become bullies or victims themselves. Encourage your child to pick friends wisely—perhaps by looking for *middle group* pals who will be true companions even when the going gets tough.

LAW #25

The Law of Earning versus Entitlement:

Teach the Work Ethic

If you believe that kids just naturally grow up demonstrating good frustration tolerance, perseverance, and self-discipline, think again. *All* of these character traits are *learned*—and must be taught by their parents. Want to guarantee that your kid will develop a good work ethic and not cut and run when the going gets tough? Here's how to lead your child's development into a responsible, self-sufficient adult.

Remember, perhaps not long ago, when you were anticipating your child's birth? All the good thoughts poured in—how cute he would be, the selection of not-overused-yet-not-too-weird names you were considering, and how brilliant this offspring was destined to be. Okay, the baby is born, the nursery is decorated, you've finally figured out how to work the Diaper Genie, and little by little you even rediscover what sleep is. As brand-new parents, you probably faced some child-rearing issues, such as whether the baby will be allowed to cuddle in your bed if he awakens and cries during the night, or maybe you talked over toilet training or preschool choices in your early parenting discussions. So far, so good, but did the issue of how to foster your child's work ethic happen to come up? You're probably thinking "What, are you nuts? Let's just get through this baby and toddler thing before we tackle that!"

Most parents are so absorbed with getting through the day sane and in one piece that it's difficult to focus on something as nebulous as the *work ethic*. The fact is, many folks either assume that the kid will naturally develop the ability to work hard, tolerate frustrating circumstances, and develop adequate self-control, or they flat-out don't even think about it.

But I can't be emphatic enough—don't put this off any longer!

Daily in my clinical practice I see parents who have made the mistake of not taking the time and attention to teach their children to be workers and achievers. These kids have learned to settle for less rather than to face and challenge adversity, to become whiners rather than creative problem solvers, and to blame others for perceived slights and lack of success. This is seen in their shoddy schoolwork, inconsistent chore and task completion, and general irresponsibility. Trying to get Junior to complete his homework or to clean up his room becomes a major hassle, often resulting in a daily family drama including Mom's nagging and Dad's reprimands. "Where did we go wrong?" is heard as a chorus of laments when folks finally realize that their kids' ability to tackle adversity, to postpone immediate gratification, and to work hard for what they desire has not occurred. Sadly, these are kids who often equate *wanting* with *getting*.

How to avoid this dilemma (or reverse it if it has already become habit) revolves around your own attitude toward work and issues of reward and entitlement. If your folks tended to give to you unconditionally (you didn't have to earn your privileges or unnecessary possessions), then perhaps you're raising your kids in the same manner. On the other hand, perhaps you grew up in a home where money was tight and you had to make do with very little. Often parents who felt deprived as children themselves vow to give their own kids as much as they can, not wanting them to be teased by peers for worn or out-of-style clothes. Not only does your son feel on top of the world when you purchase his first car for him, but you're proud that you've provided for him in a way that even your own folks couldn't. At least *he* won't be riding the bus to school, having to sit with a bunch of freshmen and sophomores during his senior year!

Although your intentions may be noble, the result is often disastrous. And it's often the kid who is the one who pays in the long run. Children who are raised with a feeling of entitlement—that the world revolves around them and that they are exempt from doing chores and taking responsibility—often grow to be adults who are bitter and resentful. Why? Didn't their parents provide everything for them? Yes and no. They provided and gave too much in one sense—too many freedoms, privileges, and things. Yet they didn't provide enough of the building blocks of the work ethic—teaching the child to postpone gratification by saving up her own money, confirming that wanting is different from needing, and that success and achievement are based on facing challenges and persevering.

You have to realize that even if you keep catering to your child's whims, the real world certainly isn't going to. And he'll begin to feel the sting of that reality as he butts heads with peers who won't cave in to his tantrums on the playground, or teachers who can't be talked into forgiving incomplete homework just because of his adorable dimples. Your home truly is the training ground for the playground, the classroom, and the workplace. The expectations that you demand will set the stage for how well your child adjusts to the expectations outside of the home. By teaching your kids to deal with frustrations appropriately, perhaps by having them share the financial responsibility for buying sneakers that are beyond your means or your good judgment, they learn that they must contribute in order to receive. That's the essence of the *behavior-consequence connection* (Law #5), the lesson that you get what you earn. Treating a kid to unnecessarily expensive sneakers without the child chipping in (even if you can afford them) sends the wrong message—that what you want, you get, even if what you want is unreasonable or even if you haven't earned it.

No one is born with the work ethic. Study after study has shown that perseverance, self-discipline, and frustration tolerance—the bases of a solid work ethic—are learned, not innate. There's no passing the buck here, blaming your child's procrastination or feeling of entitlement on your partner's or Grandma's genetic makeup just won't cut it. It's up to you, the parent, to instill the difference between *wanting* and *getting*, and to teach your child to postpone gratification in order to accomplish and succeed later as an adult.

Reasonable Expectations by Developmental Stage

Here's how to grow these expectations with your child.

Two-Year-Olds

Between 24 and 36 months of age, your child develops the ability to handle many behavioral responsibilities. Use a timer to motivate your child to clean up specific toys and put them back in their proper place before the buzzer goes off. Make chore completion fun and be sure to help out, modeling the good behavior yourself. Be careful at the grocery store that you don't cave in and buy a toy that your little one puts into the cart—that's an easy habit to start and a difficult one to get rid of!

Three-Year-Olds

Between 3 and 4 years of age children are able to perform daily chores such as putting dirty clothes in a hamper (you may want to play beat-the-buzzer or dunk-the-basketball to get them moving on this) and helping you to make their beds. Threes can fill pet bowls, pull up their own elastic-waist pants and skirts, and brush their teeth with your guidance. Praise your child for a good effort—little ones thrive on positive attention, and they don't need constant treats to motivate a good performance.

Four-Year-Olds

Fours continue to be able to complete chore responsibilities such as putting their dirty dishes on the counter or clothes in the hamper, giving the dog water or food, washing themselves in the bath with your supervision, brushing their teeth with your guidance, and picking out their clothes for the next day. Remember to thank them for their help and note that because the child was quick to get ready in the morning, there's now time to play a word game before leaving for preschool.

Early Grade Schoolers

Fives can prepare themselves for kindergarten in the morning (getting clothes out, etc.) and work 15 minutes at a time on letters, dot-to-dots, and other preacademic tasks. Fives are able to help to make their own simple lunches, dress themselves, and begin to learn to tie their shoes.

They can also begin to help younger siblings with dressing and other tasks. These children can help clean up after their baths (hanging up the towel, putting dirty clothes in the hamper), as well as making their own beds.

Six- and 7-year-olds can work cooperatively with you on homework as well as doing some of it themselves. They can put their clean clothes in the correct drawers or hang them up in the closet, pick up their bedroom daily, and meet deadlines for baths and bedtime. Early grade schoolers can be expected to brush their teeth by themselves, answer the telephone, and respond politely when spoken to. They can help with dinner chores and take out their own articles from the car each day and put them away. Many early grade schoolers can set their alarm clocks (with adult supervision) and wake up by the alarm in the morning (again, with your guidance).

Be careful not to buy on impulse or demand for your early grade schooler. Begin an allowance system and teach them to have goals. Let them see how close they are to earning a new action figure or video game. Encourage waiting and saving.

Older Grade Schoolers

Eight-, 9-, 10-, and 11-year-olds can continue with self-hygiene chores and be totally responsible for getting ready for school. Although they will need help and guidance with homework, they can do much of it on their own. These kids can bring in the mail and take out and bring in the trashcans. They can be expected to keep their rooms clean and to help out with family chores such as dusting, straightening the family and play rooms, and helping to put away laundry other than their own. Setting and clearing the table are appropriate responsibilities, as are pet chores.

Instead of giving these kids toys, treats, or possessions when demanded, have them learn to save their allowances for purchases. Teach them to buy on sale and to budget. Have them wait a few days before impulsively making a purchase—let them see that they may change their mind and be glad that they saved their money. Have them contribute at times to the rental fee for a video game or movie. Start a bank account and show them how to balance it each month.

Middle Schoolers

Twelve-, 13- and 14-year-olds are quite capable of helping out with just about everything around the house. They can cook, help clean, do yard work, and wash the car. They can be totally responsible for doing their own laundry. Encourage babysitting younger siblings and doing pet chores. Watch out that you are not doing too much for them, as they will continue to be "helpless" if you allow that. Self-esteem is largely based in accomplishment, and kids who "do" feel good about themselves.

Encourage an allowance system for purchases such as CDs, video games, and movies. Kids this age can be placed on a clothing allowance system—which teaches budgeting and planning ahead. They'll learn that "wanting" doesn't always lead to "getting"—a great lesson to learn at this time in life.

High Schoolers

Teens can be very self-sufficient—taking care of their own laundry, ironing, helping with dinner preparation and clearing, as well as watching younger siblings. If your teen is driving a car, have her chip in for auto insurance or gas, especially if she has a paying job. Encourage her to volunteer and to help with family chores, not just her own.

If she has a paying job, eliminate the allowance, but you may still have to chip in for clothing purchases. Set a limit on what you think is reasonable, and if she has extravagant tastes, let her take up the slack and put in the difference from her own savings. Don't cave in and allow privileges or freedoms that you feel uncomfortable with just because she nags you—stand your ground if you feel that her requests are inappropriate. Remember, she's learning the work ethic and frustration tolerance—skills that will serve her well as an adult!

LIVING THE LAW

How do you set the scene for building a good work ethic? Consider the following suggestions.

Don't be a peace-at-any-price parent. Giving in to your child's whines and fusses just to keep the complaining down to a dull roar only hurts both of you. Ask yourself, "If I give in and let my preschooler get away with neglecting to feed the cat, what am I teaching him?" Remember—not doing something about inappropriate behavior is still making a statement, perhaps a lesson that you don't really mean to teach.

Set up expectations for each of your children. Make them clear and reasonable, and check to be sure that the kids follow through. If they don't, set up consistent consequences that matter to your kids so that they are more apt to complete the chores or expectations in the future.

Raise the bar. As your kids mature, expect more. Most parents don't realize *how much* kids can really do, especially little ones. We tend to think of our children as helpless, and believe me, they will not try to change that perception! Preschoolers who have the dexterity and strength to pull toys out of toy boxes have the ability to put the toys back in. They just may not have the *motivation* to do so! And that's where you come in—by modeling the toy cleanup process, playing beat-the-buzzer to complete a chore in a fun way, or holding off on a treat until the toys are back in the box. Your kid will soon get the message if you stick to your guns. And expect more initiative and quality as your children grow. You shouldn't have to remind your daughter at 8 years of age to make her bed—she knows that it has to be accomplished before coming to breakfast, but again, only if you set the rule and stick to it. By the teen years, kids can do just about any job that you can around the house, plus they have more time and energy. Expect more and you'll get more!

Consider schoolwork and homework as part of the foundation for a good work ethic. Sure, your son may not be enthralled with his math homework, but he should do it without a hassle, in a timely manner, and correctly. I'm not suggesting perfection by any means, but a good, solid effort and organization are reasonable to expect when it comes to school responsibilities.

Be especially careful with a smart kid who gets by easily. Often children who are very bright find that they can succeed in school with very little effort. Challenge such a child by placing him in advanced programs if possible, or provide creative work for him yourself. Gifted, unmotivated children often find it difficult to rise to the occasion when they find themselves in truly challenging situations later in life. And because they haven't had to work hard for their accomplishments, they often give up easily when frustrated.

Start chores and responsibilities early in life. It's much easier to begin a good habit with a 3-year-old than to break a bad habit with a 13-year-old.

Decide whether your child should receive an allowance for performing his chores. Should the allowance be given for completing everyday items (picking up his room, putting away his laundry) or should it be for "extras" such as washing the car or the windows? This is an individual family decision that should be based upon what you believe teaches the best lessons to your kids.

Encourage volunteering. Studies resoundingly confirm that kids who help others, such as reading to the elderly in a nursing home, babysitting children at Sunday school, or serving food at a local soup kitchen, not only benefit others but encourage a sense of pride in the volunteer.

Help your teen to land a paying job when the time is right. In considering jobs, be sure that the workplace is a safe environment and that the job doesn't interfere with his school or homework responsibilities. Discuss how he is to handle his salary—putting some away for future purchases or responsibilities (car insurance), while keeping some for weekly spending money. When a teen receives a salary, the allowance is usually no longer necessary.

Model a positive work attitude yourself. If you work within the home, show pride in your accomplishments and how you provide a nice environment for your family. If you work outside the home, share your experiences, opportunities, and insights with your kids. Let them see that a career is not just work, it's an opportunity to grow, to access financial stability, to meet and make friends, and is an interesting place to be.

Let your kids see that just because you want something, you don't necessarily get it. Share with them the pros and cons about buying something on credit versus saving and purchasing it with cash in the future. Learn to tolerate the frustration of postponing your own gratification, and your kids will follow suit.

CONCLUSION

Raising responsible kids is one of the toughest jobs around—a balancing act between giving in and getting tough. Often it seems easier to cave in to our children's demands, to cater to their whims, and to just pick up their stuff for them. I know; I've been there and have experienced the tug on my heart. It's not easy to deny your child a new toy or article of clothing, or to stick to a definite playtime or curfew. It's much, much easier to give in, especially if it quiets them down, is accompanied with confessions of love, or just brings a few moments of peace and quiet.

But child rearing is certainly not a momentary process. And, as you already know, it's rarely easy. The responsibility for, and involvement with, your kids goes on well into adulthood. It just doesn't magically terminate as soon as they hit their 18th birthday. In fact, some of the most important decisions of their lives are made in the late teens and early adult years. Choices as to colleges, vocations, spouses, and financial responsibilities are at the forefront during this time. Kids who have solid relationships with their parents tend to make the wisest choices, since they can bounce ideas off their folks and receive the benefit of the experience gained throughout their parents' lives.

By understanding and following the 25 laws described and discussed in this book, and actually living the laws provided in each chapter, you will achieve the type of rapport with your children that will establish respectful, honest, and open relationships throughout their childhood, adolescence, and adult years.

With Law #1, your family code of values establishes ethics and mores to live by, not only now, but later as parents themselves. The passing on to a new generation of values such as honesty, respect for others, and responsibility is quite a heritage, and you should be proud that you can be a part of that intergenerational process. In Law #25, you have helped them to develop self-discipline and frustration tolerance—perhaps the greatest gifts that can be given to children. And with all the other Laws of Parenting in between, you have the necessary tools for keeping your kids well behaved and on track for future success.

Even if you have found that some of the laws are tough for you to institute, perhaps because it isn't "in your nature" to do so, just go ahead, *fake it until you make it*. If you lack patience, count to 10 before reacting. If you abuse substances yourself, decrease your dependence as you ask your children to abstain. If you haven't volunteered a day in your life, don't worry about it, but don't wait any longer. Make that phone call today and sign up the kids as well as yourself to help out at the homeless shelter or the church bazaar.

It doesn't matter whether you have experience with praising appropriately, snooping effectively, creating and employing catastrophic consequences—just do it, starting today. You'll see that over time these behaviors become second nature, especially when the payoff becomes evident. Your family life will be more comfortable and peaceful, as well as devoid of nightly dramas such as nagging and hassling the kids to get moving to hit the showers and toothbrushes. They'll just do it, because they know that you mean business and will follow through with consequences that really matter.

As I began this book with Mitchell and Cecelia's sticky situation, I end with a pleasant update on the family. Mitchell has been dumped by his girlfriend and experienced the pain of a broken heart. I feel for the kid—he's really a nice guy. But instead of taking it out on his mother and younger brother, Mitchell came in to see me to discuss the best ways to handle his emotions. It's not unusual for a kid to call or to come in on his own volition, but I never expected that from Mitchell. As you remember, I was definitely not his favorite person at the time that we first were introduced!

Instead of still being the negative, noncommunicative, and flat-out nasty kid I met many months ago, Mitchell had changed. He really wanted to talk about his feelings. Although both his pride and heart were hurt, he was able to see that it probably was for the best that he was moving on in his love life. Sure, the breakup wasn't his decision—actually the hussy had fallen for a 10th grader with his own car. There was no way that Mitchell, now in 9th grade, could measure up to that. But he did agree that he needed a diversion to keep his mind off his lousy love life and agreed to join the high school wrestling team. He met with the coach the week before school started, and even though he was kind of scrawny, he was impressive with his quick moves as well as tenacity. Mitchell is now seeded first in his weight class and becoming a leader on the wrestling team. Because he has to keep his grades up to remain in high-school athletics, the kid is actually studying and turning in his homework.

Cecelia is thrilled with Mitchell's successes, but most of all with his newfound optimism. He could have chosen a different path—to blame the girlfriend for his lousy feelings, to fail in class, and to become disengaged and disenchanted with high school. Instead, though, Mitchell decided to step up to the plate, bolstered by his own resolve as well as Cecelia's encouragement and support. And, boy, is he ever a winner. I have a very good feeling about this kid and the future that lies ahead for him—academically and socially, as well as in his family relationships. And to think it all began about a year ago with that exceptionally rude salutation. Go figure!

Maybe you don't have a Mitchell living under your roof. But if you do, or if there's a Mitchell-in-waiting lurking inside your child, waiting to burst out into a full-blown parenting headache, stop the downward slide right now. You can—and you must—invest your time, attention, and guts in following through with the ideas presented in this book. Have the insight, consistency, and perhaps most important, the love for your kids to do what's right.

I wish you the best as you find success in laying down the law!

INDEX

Underscored page references indicate boxed text.